Easy & Elegant Rose Design

Beyond the Garden

Library of Congress Cataloging-in-Publication Data

Platt, Ellen Spector.

Easy and elegant rose design: beyond the garden / Ellen Spector Platt.

   p. cm.

ISBN 1-55591-476-4 (pbk. : alk. paper)

1. Rose arrangements. 2. Floral decorations. 3. Roses. I. Title.

SB449.3.R67P58 2004

745.92--dc22

2004012370

ISBN 1-55591-476-4

Printed in China

0 9 8 7 6 5 4 3 2 1

Editorial:
   Faith Marcovecchio, Katie Raymond

Design:
   Ann W. Douden

Cover image:
   Alan and Linda Detrick

Fulcrum Publishing
16100 Table Mountain Parkway, Suite 300
Golden, Colorado 80403
(800) 992-2908 • (303) 277-1623
www.fulcrum-books.com

Beyond the Garden

Easy & Elegant Rose Design

ELLEN SPECTOR PLATT

photographs by
ALAN DETRICK

FULCRUM PUBLISHING
Golden, Colorado

Beyond the Garden

Dedication

For Our Rosebuds:

Emma Lynne Sardy, Lucy Katrina Platt,
and Annabelle Rose Platt

A lovely being, scarcely formed or moulded,
A rose with all its sweetest leaves yet folded.
— Lord Byron, Don Juan

Contents

Introduction

YOU MAY HAVE A MAGNIFICENT ROSE GARDEN

surrounding your home, with hybrid teas, climbers, standards, and shrub roses. Or you may live in an apartment and pick up a dozen peach roses as you leave the grocery store. You may receive gift roses on your birthday in an amount that matches your age. Whether you have bridal flowers you want to preserve, potpourris you want to concoct, a wreath or a wall hanging you want to craft, or a special event you need to prepare for, you'll find easy and elegant suggestions in this book.

Making sure you have the materials on hand is usually the most time-consuming part of any design. If you have the clippers, knife, wire, or foam, if you have the wreath frame, shadow box, the right ribbon or vase, the rest seems to fall into place. These designs are suggestions for displays using fresh and dried roses. Substitute and change them at will to make each craft your own. And refer to Chapter 9 for the best methods to care for fresh roses, and for drying and preserving them.

Some designs in this book use roses alone, some feature roses in combination with other materials, and in some designs, the roses provide merely an accent. The decision on how many roses to use is sometimes aesthetic, but more often practical. How many roses do I have available at any given time? Will I buy to supplement the flowers in my garden? Will I use only what I have?

I recently gave up my farm where I grew hundreds of varieties of flowers and herbs in cutting gardens. Mostly these were for drying and selling either by the bunch or in wreaths and arrangements. My shrubs and vines provided a never-ending source of accent and filler materials. I grew roses to dry and add as focal points to my designs. Now I'm in an apartment in New York City where I purchase flowers from florists or green markets. I beg and borrow from friends when I need something extra. Visiting my grown children in New England, I invariably arrive home with branches of blue juniper with berries, brilliant winterberry, bittersweet in coils. I "borrow" Queen Anne's lace, goldenrod, and purple loosestrife from roadsides and fields to make commercially grown flowers look less formal and more spontaneous. I want to re-create the garden look even when I no longer have the garden. The designs in this book span my farm and apartment periods. Many of the flowers are from my own garden, others are purchased. As always I love the challenge of doing the best with what I have.

IN 1986 the U.S. Congress passed a bill declaring the rose to be the national flower of the United States. The official proclamation signed by Ronald Reagan noted that roses grow in all fifty states and that our first president, George Washington, bred them. The rose won out over the daisy, marigold, lilac, and other garden flowers to receive this designation. Four states and the Canadian province of Alberta have chosen the rose as their symbol—not just cultivated roses, but the wild prairie rose or the Cherokee rose growing locally. The storied White House rose garden is the site for receiving foreign dignitaries and signing legislation.

Roses symbolize peace, respect, love, and elegance; the red rose passion, the white rose purity. Sixteen long-stemmed pink roses celebrate a sixteenth birthday; fifty yellow roses, a golden anniversary. A bouquet of red roses on February 14th has only one meaning: Be mine!

A bunch of dead roses on the same day means, "Drop dead! I never want to see you again!" In the floral industry, roses represent over a fifth of the sales nationally.

In poetry, song, and literature, the flowering of the rose is a metaphor for life; from the rosebud to its dropped petals, from roses blooming in the cheeks to their perfume wafting on the air, authors, lyricists, and poets claim roses as their own.

GARDENERS are the most generous people on earth, ready to share advice, cuttings, seeds, divisions, and flowers. Whoever we asked welcomed us into their gardens and homes to photograph. When I requested extra stems for a vase, I was given permission to wield my clippers at will. When I needed rose hips for

an arrangement, they were on my doorstep the next morning in a FedEx box, straight from Plum Island, Massachusetts. Photographer Alan Detrick and I extend our particular thanks for the generosity of Lorraine and Don Jones, Ellen and Gordon Remer, Paulette and John Lee, Barbara Gill, Rita Catlin, Ruth Flounders, Mort Haefitz, and all those who offered their favorite tips, expertise, recipes, and props, especially Karlton Holmes, Ellen Zachos, Steve Bach, Dolores Delin, and Gladys Santee.

Shrubs and plants were sent to us for trial by David Austin Roses Inc., the Conard Pyle Company, Ecke Bros., and Susan McCoy at Garden Media Group. When my work life involves trying new varieties of plants and evaluating them for home and garden use, I know I've been blessed.

And I am also blessed to have a daughter, Jen Hopkins, who specializes both in gardening and the law. She helps me with contractual and copyright matters from her office in Concord, New Hampshire, then runs home to Canterbury to tend her vegetables.

We are extremely grateful to Linda Detrick whose name appears in no prominent spot in this book but whose hand, heart, and soul make their presence felt throughout, in every design and in every photo.

And as always, my greatest appreciation goes to my dear friend Ben Platt, who spots the wild things, brakes for flower emergencies, sniffs out the lavender, and finds the roses wherever we go.

Beyond the Garden

*The wilderness and the solitary place shall be glad for them;
and the desert shall rejoice and blossom like a rose.
It shall blossom abundantly and rejoice even with joy and singing.*

— Old Testament, Isaiah 35:1–2

Red roses and
calla lillies grace
this purple
goblet.

Introduction

Beyond the Garden

Simple Arrangements: Roses & Friends

Gather therefore the rose whilst yet is prime
For soon comes age that will her pride deflower
Gather the Rose of Love, whilst yet is time …

Roses red and violets blew,
And all the sweetest flowers
that in the garden grew.

— Edmund Spenser, The Faerie Queene

From the tightly furled rosebud to the swelling fleshy rose hip, each stem at each stage has its own beauty. One stem can stand alone in an etched crystal vase or a modest glass test tube. Massed stems in a silver urn or an old watering can need no companions. You can mix cut roses of any color, size, or shape to capture the beauty of the garden and create an informal bouquet.

Those times when you have but a few roses and want to mix them with other garden flowers, almost any combination works. Here are some examples to prove the point.

Chapter 1

Stuff-It-in-a-Vase

When I make a floral arrangement at home to please only myself, my favorite type of arrangement is "Stuff-It-in-a-Vase": masses of one type of flower stuffed in an interesting container. No worry about "design" or "creativity," because the impact of the blooms speaks for itself. With roses, there is often a bonus of a heavenly aroma as the flowers unfurl.

Please note that when you stuff roses in a vase they will last longer if they're in water with floral preservative rather than in floral foam. (See pp. 118–120, "Caring for Fresh Roses"). I keep a stock of containers in my cupboard, everything from teapots and odd china sugar bowls to white metal posy holders, unusual baskets with plastic liners, crystal cachepots, and ceramic vases. I have a good excuse for meandering at a flea market, antique show, or garage sale, because I might find the perfect size or color container for my next display. Chips and dents can usually be turned away or camouflaged by foliage, so there are bargains to be had. For dried flowers even cracked containers may be perfect.

Early Summer Rose Bowl

One fine day late in June I've cut a sampling from each rosebush in bloom. Some stems are fully opened, others are in bud. The flat blossoms of 'Mediland Pink' single roses stand out from the others because of their pink-and-white combination and their flat form. A pin holder or frog attached to the bottom of the old pewter container with some floral clay holds the stems in place. Stems are all cut short, and a few leaves are included. I've even managed to find a place for the deep-red rose that sprang up from rootstock when one of my hybrid roses died back completely. (See previous page for a photo of this arrangement.)

Fall Rose Bowl

In autumn, roses often have a spurt of rebloom. The warmth of the copper teapot used as a container helps set the autumn mood. In addition to the collection of roses, I've used the coral rose hips from the same 'Pink Meidiland' rose seen in the summer arrangement, and I've included the smaller hips from the wild multiflora rose. Because the mouth of the teapot is small, this arrangement needs no mechanical supports. Stems of the roses are all cut short, no more than six to eight inches long, and placed in water with floral preservative.

As petals fall from roses past their prime, I leave the dropped petals to become part of the display.

Roses with Others

These combinations were dictated not by design considerations but by what's blooming in the garden.

Pretty in pink: 'Pink Meidiland' rose and astilbe.

Astilbe

I could spare some pink astilbe from the border in front of the house, so I followed through with a monochromatic arrangement of all different shades of pink roses. An all-white or all-peach arrangement would be equally charming. See p. 58 (Lemonade) for a monochromatic arrangement in shades of yellow.

A romantic combination of pastels.

Campanula

The purple bellflower (*Campanula glomerata*) was just starting to bloom, so I cut five stems that were distributed among the multicolored roses. In the wide-mouth glass container, I used clear marbles to hold the stems in place.

For Flag Day; red, white, and blue

Veronica

Very few flowers are as true blue as the *Veronica* 'Crater Lake Blue.' When this delicate perennial blooms in the cutting garden, it seems to demand to be in combination with red and white flowers. I bought this porcelain vegetable dish for a song at a flea market because it was missing its lid. Its delicate blue pattern makes a perfect foil for the combination of the rose 'Europeana,' Kousa dogwood, and veronica. Again, all stems are cut short and held by a pin holder attached with floral clay to the base of the container. Or substitute white peonies for Kousa dogwood; they bloom at the same time.

Just a few stems of a miniature rose make a lovely small arrangement.

Small Things

God gave us memory that we
might have roses in December

—James Barrie

At Christmas I no more
desire a rose
Than wish snow in May's
new-fangled mirth;
But like of each thing that in
season grows.

—William Shakespeare,
Love's Labour's Lost

Pile up the pots of 'Sunblaze'
miniatures for an instant centerpiece.

Sometimes in December, January, or February, when I'm expecting guests, I want not just the memory of flowers but a centerpiece of actual roses displayed in the easiest possible way.

Dig out a wide soup tureen or large pottery fruit bowl from the back of the cupboard where it's been lurking, and examine its colors and the size of its opening. Then go to the supermarket or garden center and buy five to seven pots of 'Sunblaze' miniature roses in plastic pots. Purchase varieties that will complement the container; these two are 'Sweet Concertina' and 'Candy.' Come home, water them, and pile them in the container. You may need to put something in the bottom to elevate the center pot. Insert the others slightly at an angle. Remember that this is for show for a night or two, up to a week. Enjoy your party, then remove the pots and place them on a windowsill with bright light, add saucers, and treat them as houseplants for the rest of the winter. Deadhead blooms as they die. Come late spring, plant out in the garden near the front of a border where they will develop into small shrubs. What a bargain!

Treat the pots of miniature 'Sunblaze' roses as a source for cut flowers. Cut the stems in bud or blossom and use them in a grouping of miniature vases or in one container with several openings. Here they are placed in a reproduction of an antique inkwell, which holds water. You'll find many places in your home that will be enhanced by this inexpensive, simple, yet charming arrangement.

Yes, the treatment may destroy the plant, but it will serve a new function on the compost pile. Get over it!

In mid-spring, when perennials are bursting into bloom, you may have just a few stems of each that you're willing to cut. Place each species in its own small container; volunteer bachelor's buttons in a demitasse cup, two sunny *Centaurea macrocephala* in egg cups, lavender in a sake pot, a handful of heritage roses in a creamer, and the delphinium in a metal basket, rescued from the clutches of a groundhog. Move the containers into a pleasing configuration to finish the arrangement.

Hearts and Flowers

Convey a sentimental message of love with a heart-shaped container and the old-fashioned color of roses. The paler lavender is enlivened by a jolt of bright purple statice and hot pink mini carnations.

The container is nothing but a cardboard box sprayed with some silver paint from the hardware store. What once was a dull tan is now a glowing silver.

Keep the flowers in this arrangement short and tightly controlled to maintain the heart shape of the container.

WHAT YOU NEED

12–15 lavender roses

1 bunch mini carnations

9 stems purple statice

floral preservative

heart-shaped container measuring 9" at its widest point

silver spray paint (optional)

heavy-duty aluminum foil

1 block floral foam

paring knife

floral shears

WHAT YOU DO

1 Condition the flowers in water with floral preservative for at least six hours. See instructions on pp. 118–120.

2 Meanwhile spray-paint the heart-shaped container if desired.

3 Line the container with heavy-duty aluminum foil. The object is to make it waterproof. If you're lucky enough to have a china heart, this step won't be necessary.

4 Cut the floral foam to fit the container using the largest pieces possible, coming close to the edges.

5 Soak the foam in water containing floral preservative, mixed according to package directions, for at least thirty minutes. Then replace the foam in the lined container.

6 Trim the stems to three or four inches, cutting each flower as you need it. Place the roses around the rim of the heart as shown, leaving some space between them. Then start to fill in with the carnations.

7 Add more roses in the next ring toward the center, inserting them so they are slightly higher than the outer ring of flowers. Keep filling in with roses and carnations.

8 Cut the statice and tuck in around the arrangement, filling in any spaces using an irregular pattern.

9 Continue to add water carefully to this arrangement every day to keep it healthy. When the roses die, pull the statice and dry for potpourri or other uses.

TIP:

The cost of this design is reduced by the choice of statice and mini carnations as adjuncts to the roses. Substituting other companions such as anemones or sweetheart roses will be beautiful but will raise the cost of the project.

Short and Sweet

It's midwinter and I'm starved for flowers indoors. The only thing blooming is one ungainly amaryllis flower, falling over on its tall stalk, a gift plant where it was definitely the thought that counted. There are also a few stems of the quince I cut two weeks ago that are finally forced into bloom. I buy a bunch of lavender roses, a bunch of purple anemones, a bunch of fragrant hyacinth, and I am charmed with the results.

Beyond the Garden

1 stem amaryllis

10 roses

10 stems anemone

8 stems hyacinth

a few stems quince

floral preservative

1 block floral foam

footed bowl (this one is $5\frac{1}{2}$" x $7\frac{1}{2}$")

paring knife

floral tape

floral shears

WHAT YOU DO

1 Condition the flowers. See pp. 118–120 for instructions. Soak the foam in water to which you've added preservative, according to package directions.

2 Cut the foam to fit the container. The foam should reach almost edge to edge and be about two inches higher than the rim. Tape in place.

3 Place the amaryllis first, top center. You will need to cut the stem to about four inches. Insert the stem one inch deep into the foam and leave there. The other flowers will go around and under the amaryllis bloom.

4 Insert the roses next around the rim. The stems should be cut short, to about three inches. Estimate the placement before you start so they are evenly distributed.

5 Place the anemones between the roses, also cutting them so their stems are short. Then insert the hyacinth in the tier between the roses and the amaryllis.

6 Cut the quince or other filler into short pieces and fill in any gaps in the arrangement.

7 Continue to add water to the foam every day until it's time to say good-bye. Because the stems are short they will last longer in the foam than long-stemmed flowers would. The life-giving water has less distance to travel to reach the flower head.

TIP:

Amaryllis have hollow stems. Make sure your first placement in the foam is where you want it. After you place it in the foam, don't remove and reinsert it. If you do, the plug of foam in the hollow stem will prevent the uptake of water.

Simple Arrangements

Double Delight

Double delight is both the name of a favorite hybrid tea rose and a favorite design style. The rose itself is cream and pink flushed with carmine, blooming from late spring until fall with a heady aroma. It dries beautifully. 'Double Delight' is a garden rose, rarely seen in the floral trade. For this arrangement I chose unnamed white and blush peach roses from the florist.

Doubling a simple design packs a power punch, especially when a small, single arrangement would get dwarfed by its background. Repetition gives more than twice the impact, just as two children are more than twice the work of one. Anytime you can double or even triple a design for display, you enhance its interest.

WHAT YOU NEED

30 roses, multicolor or in two contrasting colors

floral preservative

2 hanging baskets or other containers (these are made of tin)

2 strong plastic baggies if your containers are unlined

1 brick floral foam

paring knife

floral shears

ribbon

2 tacks or 2 wreath hangers

WHAT YOU DO

1 Condition the roses in a bucket of warm water (see pp. 118–120 for instructions). I made these arrangements when the flowers had partially opened. If the flowers are still in bud when you arrange them, don't crowd the roses; allow them space to open fully.

2 Soak the foam in water to which floral preservative has been added according to package instructions.

3 Hang the baskets. Instead of wreath hangers I put two tacks in the top surface of the cupboard door and hung the ribbon from the tack, suspending the baskets from it.

4 Insert a plastic baggie in each basket.

5 Cut the wet floral foam to fit. It *must* peep about an inch above the rim of the basket.

6 Divide the roses in half so you don't run out before completing the second design. Cut stems as you insert each flower into the foam. The stems should be short so as not to hide the handle—two to five inches of stem at most. The foam rises above the rim of the basket so the bottom front and bottom side roses can be inserted at an angle.

7 If working with two colors of roses, scatter them at random. Push a few flowers a little deeper into the foam so the arrangement does not have a "flat" look.

TIP:

Whenever you want flowers or leaves to droop down over the sides, make the foam higher than the container, so you can insert the stem up into the foam with the flower hanging down. By breaking the plane of the rim, you merge the roses and the basket, making the arrangement appear to be an organic whole rather than two separate elements.

8 Add two or three stems with leaves attached in any bare spots. Go on to the next arrangement. I try to make them approximately the same but not identical, as I find that goal almost impossible to attain. I console myself with the thought that Mother Nature never repeats herself.

TIP:

With a long-spouted watering can add water to the arrangement every day. Flowers whose stems are very short usually last much longer in foam than long-stemmed flowers, so you may be pleasantly surprised.

Simple Arrangements

Wreaths

She wore a wreath of roses
The night that first we met.
—Thomas Haynes Bayly

Wreaths have served as symbols since ancient times and in many cultures, representing life, regeneration, rebirth, and fertility, as well as death, mourning, and sacrifice. Wreaths also symbolize glory, victory, and happiness. In Greek and Roman times, the laurel or olive wreath signified wisdom. Starting in the seventh century B.C., laurel wreaths were bestowed upon the winners of contests for music, poetry, and athletics in the Panhellenic games. Olive wreaths were awarded at the Olympic games and ivy wreaths were awarded for drama. Roman emperors wore wreaths of roses.

Chapter 2

Beyond the Garden

Wreaths appear in decorations on sixteenth-century Chinese silver, an eighteenth-century Ottoman cradle, and Christian prayer books. Hadassah, the Jewish organization in support of Israel, chose the myrtle wreath as its symbol.

In the current culture in the United States, a wreath on the front door extends a welcome to all who see it. Many Christian homes display wreaths of evergreens in December. Floral wreaths crown the heads of brides and bridesmaids, and wreaths stand sentinel at gravesites and memorial statues.

Wreaths come in all shapes, sizes, colors, and materials. The rose wreaths pictured in this chapter feature fresh and dried roses, buds, hips, and canes. In some of the wreaths, roses have the starring role; in others, roses are part of the supporting cast or even bit players among other flowers and herbs. Adapt any of the designs to fit your space, décor, and available flowers.

When you make a rose wreath, you are participating in a tradition that stretches back more than 2,500 years.

Wreaths

Ring-around-a-Rosie

Company is expected for dinner tomorrow evening. I want an easy but impressive centerpiece. On a beautiful day in midsummer, I wander into the cutting garden to search for flowers. I cut whatever is available, from lowly marigolds and zinnias to globe thistles and lilies. There are but a few roses, most in bud; they get harvested as well, on short stems because that's all I'll need. The foliage I select is mountain mint for its color and the freshest aroma imaginable. The casual combination of flowers captures the essence of summer.

WHAT YOU NEED

An assortment of fresh flowers and herbs: marigold, zinnia, globe thistle, white coneflower, veronica, yarrow, lily, rose, mountain mint, or whatever you have. Use more foliage to compensate for fewer flowers. Cut them in bud as well as in full bloom.

floral preservative

large floral foam ring with plastic backing, 12" in diameter

small lazy Susan (optional)

floral shears

Beyond the Garden

18

WHAT YOU DO

1 Condition the flowers for six hours or more (see pp. 118–120).

2 Soak the foam ring in water mixed with floral preservative for about thirty minutes. The sink is a good place for this. Remove and wipe the plastic dry.

3 Place on the lazy Susan for ease of construction, spinning as necessary to work around all sides.

4 If you want to feature the roses and have only a few, save them for last. Start with one kind of flower that you have a lot of, cut the stems to two inches, and insert all around the foam, turning the form as you continue. Make sure you insert flowers on the top, the sides, and the inside of the ring.

5 The aim is to cover all the foam with flowers. Work with flowers in size order, starting with the biggest. The first flower to be added were the lilies. Then I added the globe thistle because they were abundant. Save the smallest and the most precious for last, adding them where they will be most visible.

6 The only trick here is to keep the stems short, two to three inches at most.

7 This wreath should last for about a week if the flowers are fresh and they are well conditioned. You must take the wreath to the sink and add water to the foam every day, drying off the plastic bottom before returning to the place of honor.

Centerpiece or hanging wreath: you choose.

VARIATION ON A THEME
Many wreaths can serve as both centerpiece and door decoration, and that is particularly true here. This wreath can be hung on a sturdy nail on a door for an unusual welcome to your home, though it needs a shady spot. Daily watering is particularly important if you want this wreath to last more than a day or two. After watering, hold upright over the sink to let it drain before wiping the bottom and rehanging.

TIP:
If you'll be hanging the wreath, inspect your placement of flowers while holding the wreath upright. It's easy to miss spots when you construct a wreath on a table and then view it from another perspective.

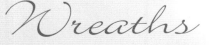

Wreaths

Beyond the Garden

Here Today ...

Prune shrub roses at the "wrong" time of year and earn yourself some long stems to make a charming fresh rose wreath. As a hardworking gardener who never has enough time to complete all the chores, I often prune when I need materials for home decorations rather than at the prescribed time of year. This philosophy applies to holly, boxwood, and all the winter evergreens, as well as to forsythia, roses, hydrangea, and other flowering shrubs.

This wreath combines a favorite old shrub rose, 'Ferdie,' with the wild multiflora rose that springs up uninvited on my Pennsylvania farm and throughout the East. Other areas of the country have their own wild species, such as prairie rose. Use one or two species, whatever you have, or combine one type of rose with another flower, such as Queen Anne's lace, that may be yours for the taking.

TIP:

Cut the rose stems when the buds are just starting to pop and keep the floral foam well watered each day to increase the longevity of the wreath. After the roses have faded, cut them off and keep the vine wreath base for reuse.

WHAT YOU NEED

8 stems of shrub roses, each 2–3' long, plus 3 pieces, each about 8" long

floral preservative

1 round plastic cage, 3¼" at its base, containing floral foam. Look for one that has two holes on the sides to thread wire through.

vine wreath base, round or oval, about 14" in diameter

nail or wreath hook

3' floral reel wire

wire cutters

handful of Spanish moss or green sheet moss

leather garden gloves (optional)

floral shears

WHAT YOU DO

1 Condition the shrub roses in a bucket of warm water (see pp. 118–120 for instructions).

2 Soak cage with floral foam in water for thirty minutes.

3 Hang the vine wreath base on a nail or wreath hook for the construction process, either in its final place or in your work area.

4 Cut a two-foot piece of reel wire. Place the cage at the bottom of the wreath on the front side of the wreath. Wire it in place with the reel wire, going through the two holes on the sides and making it secure.

5 Drape the moss over the cage, camouflaging it. The moss will be held in place by the flowers.

6 The basic technique is to cut each stem on a slant. Insert the longer stemmed flowers into the foam first and wind each one around the wreath. Use small pieces of reel wire to tie up any recalcitrant stems. If some of the vine base shows through the flowers and leaves, that adds to the design. Cut off any stems that are too long. After the long stems are inserted and wound around the wreath, use a few smaller pieces and fill in the area around the cage at the bottom.

On the Beach

An herb wreath features tansy, safflower, and rose hips.

These roses' season of interest extends from early summer when the buds unfurl to the middle of fall when the hips shrink and die away. I love to capture their beauty for indoor arrangements, by themselves in an old iron teapot or with other late-blooming flowers.

This wreath is unusual in two respects: it's formed in a rectangle rather than the ubiquitous circle and, while sensational fresh, the materials will dry in place giving you a wreath to enjoy all fall.

WHAT YOU NEED

24 tansy stems

15–18 safflower stems

8–10 clusters of large rose hips

42" of 16-gauge wire

wire cutters

leather garden gloves (optional)

floral shears

2 yards of floral reel wire

WHAT YOU DO

1   Fashion the 16-gauge wire into an eight-by-eleven-inch rectangle. Wrap any extra wire around the rectangle to keep it together. Remember that the wreath will gain two to three inches on each side, giving you a completed size of at least twelve by fifteen inches. (See p. 95 for a dried rose wreath that uses the same type of rectangular wire frame.)

Beach roses (*Rosa rugosa*) have fat hips as big as crab apples and beautiful wrinkled foliage. These roses are sometimes called sea tomatoes for the size and color of the hips. The hips are used in traditional jellies and herbal teas, both for the flavor and the high vitamin C content. What concerns us here is their stunning appearance in any floral design.

Beyond the Garden

2　Cut the stems of all the materials to three inches. The beach roses are very thorny and you may want to use gloves while handling them.

3　Tie the reel wire onto the wreath base at any point.

4　Make a little bunch of three or four stems, mixing the flowers at random. Wrap the bunch to the frame with two turns of the reel wire. You may have more of one type of flower, so the random technique allows you to use those more liberally. Lay another small bunch over top of the stems of the first, wrapping that in place. The wrapping technique is illustrated with another wreath of smaller rose hips on p. 25.

5　Continue around the wreath frame in this manner, always laying the new bunch on top on the stems of the prior bunch.

6　With the last bunch you may have to cut the stems a little shorter to fit them in. Cut off the reel wire and tie it off to the back of the frame.

7　If you want the wreath to dry evenly, give it a quarter turn every day as it is hanging.

TIP:

I chose the three elements in this wreath—tansy, safflower, and rose hips—because they look great fresh but will all dry in place. If you make any substitutions, look for another species that will dry just by hanging and isn't too fussy about having conditions that are too warm, dark, or dry. Hydrangea, goldenrod, and sweet Annie come immediately to mind, and all are available in late summer or early fall.

TIP:

When you make any wreath of fresh herbs or flowers, make it extra full to allow for the inevitable shrinkage that will take place as the materials dry. Pull the reel wire tightly as you go. When the stems shrink you don't want the wreath to loosen too much and fall apart.

VARIATION ON A THEME
Hips of the *Rosa rugosa* vary in size, but all are a treasure for the floral designer. Here are some featured in my favorite "Stuff it in a Vase" design.

A bunch of snowberry is enlivened by a few stems of rose hips.

Wreaths

Beyond the Garden

24

Two oval wreaths, made separately, are bound together for holiday display.

The larger arbivitae wreath won't shed no matter how long it hangs, and the smaller rose hip wreath will dry in place for the perfect long-lasting and natural holiday decoration. Rose hips, the fruit of the shrub containing the seeds, swell in the fall in many species and turn a beautiful shade of bright red. Anywhere you would use berries in wreaths or arrangements, red rose hips are a valuable addition.

These small hips come from the wild multiflora rose, whose flowers are part of the wreath on p. 20. While some farmers and homeowners see the wild multiflora as a weedy nuisance, I see it as an opportunity. These berry-like hips are small and green as they form, then ripen as any fruit does, evolving to a coral color. After a hard frost they continue to change into a soft, deep red. Pick the stems when the color is most appealing, leaving some for the birds to snack on.

WHAT YOU NEED

50–60 stems of arbivitae or other evergreens, each about 8" long

60–70 stems of small, wild rose hips, each about 5" long

4 yards 16-gauge wire

wire cutters

1 reel florist wire

floral shears

leather garden gloves (optional) for cutting the rose hips

nail or wreath hanger

bow (optional)

WHAT YOU DO

1   Make a twelve-by-nine-inch oval ring of the 16-gauge wire, using a double thickness of wire so it will be extra strong for the arbivitae stems. The finished size of the wreath will be approximately fourteen by eleven inches.

2   Make another oval ring of the 16-gauge wire, ten inches by seven inches. These are the two wreath bases.

3   Tie the end of the reel wire to the larger oval. Take a small clump of evergreen stems (three to five) and wrap them tightly to the wreath base. Then take another clump and lay it on top of the first stems, wrapping it in place with the reel wire. Two wraps of the wire will be enough for this process.

4   Continue around the wreath in this fashion. When you get back to the start, cut the reel wire and tie it off tightly in the back.

5   Take the smaller oval wire base and wrap on the rose hips in exactly the same way. Each clump will have about five stems. Wrap until you reach the beginning, then cut and tie off the reel wire.

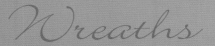

6   Lay the rose hip wreath on top of the evergreen wreath. Take the reel wire and tie them together in four places, reaching in to secure the bases to each other.

7   Hang over a nail or from a wreath hanger. With another piece of reel wire, tie on the bow at the bottom, if desired. Some will prefer to leave the wreath totally natural.

TIP:

Make the rose hip wreath extra full because the berries and greens will shrink by about 20 percent as they dry.

Beyond the Garden

VARIATION ON A THEME

- Use the rose hip oval on its own without a bow or other decoration and enjoy the minimalist style.

- Pair the rose hip oval with another oval wreath of dried materials using all goldenrod, tansy, or yarrow for a warm fall combination.

- Form the rose hip wreath in a circle rather than an oval and use it as the base of a centerpiece, as in this simple stack of bell peppers in warm colors.

- Form the rose hip wreath in a heart shape, bending the wire for the base and then wrapping as shown on p. 25.

Wreaths

Winter Rose Wreath

Make this wreath for a party or special gathering at Christmas, for Valentine's Day, or just to chase the winter blues.

Hang your wreath on an outside door if temperatures stay above freezing. Otherwise, hang it in a cool spot such as an inside door or window, rather than over a fireplace where the heat will hasten the demise of the fresh roses. If your roses were very fresh when you bought them and you allow them a long drink before making the wreath (see step 2), they will look good for five to seven days or more.

The materials in this wreath will gradually dry while hanging and continue to look attractive, if not as sprightly, as when first made. Roses will sometimes dry in place. I chose this variety, 'Mercedes,' because unlike deep-crimson roses, which dry "black," 'Mercedes' dries to a true and beautiful red.

WHAT YOU NEED

fresh-cut pine boughs

fresh eucalyptus

15 or more bright-red roses

floral shears or a sharp knife

14" vine wreath base

ribbon bow and extra 24" of ribbon

scissors

stapler

small florist water tubes with caps, one for each rose

florist reel wire

nail or wreath hook

baby's breath (optional)

WHAT YOU DO

1 Condition fresh greens by recutting stems and standing in lukewarm water for six hours.

2 Strip leaves off roses. Fill a sink with lukewarm water and immerse stems. Recut each stem on a slant underwater with a sharp floral shears or a knife. Then stand in a bucket of water as above. For best results, add floral preservative to the water according to package directions.

3 Take the vine wreath base and loop the ribbon around it. Staple the ends of the ribbon together securely. You will hang the wreath from this loop when finished.

4 Cut the greens into pieces, about eight inches long, discarding the woody stems.

5 Remove the caps from the tubes, fill with water, and recap them. Cut the roses to four to six inches and insert each stem in a tube through the hole in the cap.

6 Tie the end of the reel wire onto the vine wreath base near the ribbon loop.

7 Wrap a handful of greens onto the wreath, pulling tightly, then lay another handful over the stems of the one before. Mix pine and eucalyptus as you wrap.

Beyond the Garden

Add the roses in the same way by wrapping the tubes onto the wreath base with the reel wire.

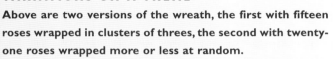

8   If a little of the vine wreath base peeks out from among the greens, it will only enhance the natural look of the wreath.

9   When you come full circle around the wreath, cut and tie off the end of the wire to the back of the wreath.

10   Hang from the ribbon loop to a hook or nail. Add the bow to cover the nail.

11   If you choose to use the optional baby's breath, tuck it in among the greens after the wreath is hanging in place.

VARIATIONS ON A THEME

Above are two versions of the wreath, the first with fifteen roses wrapped in clusters of threes, the second with twenty-one roses wrapped more or less at random.

VARIATIONS ON A THEME

You have lots of options in addition to the ones shown here: use pastel pink roses and a bright-pink bow to celebrate the winter birthday of a special little girl, white roses and a white satin bow for a winter wedding or shower. As I inserted the baby's breath in this wreath, it put me in mind of a sudden snow shower, but if you're not a fan of baby's breath, omit it. Add some small pinecones instead. Use whatever winter greens you have available. Boxwood and arborvitae are both lovely and long lasting. Or, substitute preserved eucalyptus for fresh. Scatter lots of roses about or use fewer in a more regular pattern, depending on your whim.

Ecke's Ranch in Southern California, growers of 80 to 90 percent of poinsettias sold in the United States, has hybridized a new poinsettia called 'Winter Rose.' With its rounded appearance and curled bracts it resembles a rose more than a traditional poinsettia. Poinsettias make good cut flowers and will last in water tubes for several weeks, so they work very well in this wreath in place of roses. No need to singe the cut stems as is often recommended, but keep them away from cold drafts and frost.

Construct this form of Winter Rose Wreath in the same way as the "real" rose wreath above.

Wreaths

Bed the Garden

Topiaries

What's in a name?
That which we call a rose
by any other name would smell as sweet
So Romeo would,
were not he Romeo called.

—William Shakespeare, Romeo and Juliet

Colonial Williamsburg does it, so do Longwood Gardens and Disney World: form living plants, shrubs, and trees into fantastic shapes known as *topiary*. Topiary is the art of training and trimming plants into geometric, abstract, or realistic shapes. Mazes, arches, balls, pillars, and pyramids; dinosaurs, elephants, and cowardly lions are all inspirations for the topiary designer. Boxwood and privet are favorite plants for large topiaries; ivy and rosemary for table-sized designs.

Chapter 3

Topiary designers also create massive wire or wood frameworks to support fresh-cut or dried flowers. Sometimes the framework is stuffed with moist sphagnum moss in which to root and grow annuals or ground covers. Ivy and creeping fig are perfect for this purpose. The rigidity and formality of smaller topiaries complement many styles of home décor, from the most contemporary to traditional, even Victorian interiors.

'Charles Aznavour' standard (above); 'Fuschia Meidiland' standard (right).

A rose tree or standard is a form of living topiary where the shrub is grafted atop a stout stem and pruned to bloom in a ball, a fragrant rose lollipop for the terrace. Standards are planted directly in a garden to provide height amongst shorter shrubs and perennials and are planted in tubs for terraces, balconies, and entranceways.

Here are several styles of fresh and dried topiaries that can be adapted to include many other flowers, sizes, or colors.

Lavender Tower

Create a lavender tower with any combination of dried flowers that you have in abundance, but most of them need to be spiked, with flowers growing up the stems, flaunting their color. Both larkspur and lavender fill the bill here. Add dried roses to the finished tower to show them off.

WHAT YOU NEED

10–12 bunches dried lavender

1 bunch dried larkspur

24 dried roses

14"-tall Styrofoam cone (will make a 17" tower)

3 handfuls of green sheet moss, enough to cover the cone

60–75 floral pins (also called fern pins or greening pins, they are shaped like hairpins)

lazy Susan (optional)

sturdy rubber band

floral shears

1½ –2 yards ribbon

glue gun and glue sticks

WHAT YOU DO

1   Cover the cone with sheet moss, cutting the moss as needed.

2   Pin the moss in place with a few (3–12) floral pins. Leave the bottom surface of the cone bare for best stability.

3   Place the cone on the lazy Susan while you attach the flowers. Starting at the top of the cone, pin small clusters of lavender with the stems cut to about eight inches. Allow the flowers' heads to extend above the point of the cone by three inches. Each cluster should consist of about eight stems. If you try to pin too many at one time, the pin will come loose.

4   Keep turning the cone and work down toward the bottom, pinning new clusters of lavender on top of the stems above. Try to distribute your supply of lavender evenly over the moss.

5   When you are eight inches from the bottom, stop. Slip the rubber band over the cone and position it three inches from the bottom.

6   For the last row of lavender, instead of pinning the clusters, slip the stems under the rubber band to hold them in place.

7   Add individual stems of larkspur throughout the tower. There is no need to pin them. Cut the stems short (to about three inches) and the lavender will hold it in place.

8   Add the roses last, again cutting the stems to about three inches, starting near the top and turning the tower to distribute the flowers evenly.

9   Tie the ribbon tightly over the rubber band to hide it and make a bow. The rubber band will eventually deteriorate and the ribbon will hold everything in place.

Summer Topiary

While it looks elegant enough for any formal occasion, this topiary arrangement is just a bunch of roses plunked in a vase. A bow and a few more flowers at the base are all you need to complete this very professional look. As the buds open, the topiary expands in a delightful way.

12 or more large-headed roses with
strong, straight stems

2 other flower species: here,
7 stems purple ageratum
and 7 stems green amaranth

floral preservative

vase with narrow neck (this one is
$2\frac{1}{4}$" wide at the top)

for a clear vase, glass marbles to hold
the stems; for an opaque vase,
marbles, pin holder, or a "frog" to
hold the stems

floral shears

2 sturdy rubber bands

1 yard ribbon

scissors

WHAT YOU DO

1 Condition roses (see pp. 118–120
for detailed instructions).

2 Pour half the marbles in the vase
(or place pin holder or frog).
Add water into which you've
mixed floral preservative according
to package instructions.

3 Strip all the leaves off the roses.

4 Cut stems of roses to fourteen
inches.

5 Form them into a bunch in your
hand, adding roses one at a time,
with the center flower highest and
the tops of others a little lower.

6 Wrap with a rubber band just
under the flower heads. Cut the
bottom of the stems even and
wrap with another rubber band
near the bottom of the bunch.

7 Stuff the rose bundle in the middle
of the vase. Pour the rest of the
marbles around the stems to hold
them upright.

8 Add short stems of ageratum
around the vase, just at the neck.

9 Add short stems of amaranth in
between the ageratum, allowing
the long strands to droop down in
their natural habit. The ageratum
and amaranth will fill in any gaps at
the neck and help hold the rose
bundle in place.

10 For a finishing touch, tie the
ribbon in a bow just under the
flower heads, hiding the top
rubber band. Trim the edges of the
ribbon. The other rubber band will
be hidden among the glass
marbles.

Substitute any pretty foliage for the ageratum and amaranth such as small hosta leaves or stems of boxwood. Are you growing any shrubs with variegated foliage? Some trimmings will look handsome with white or cream colored roses on a wedding table.

TIPS:

• Stems must be long for this topiary, so commercially grown roses are usually preferable. The other flowers can come straight from your garden. Select any garden flowers that complement the color of the roses or choose your roses based on the colors available in your cutting garden.

• For a larger top to the topiary ball, just use more roses, and possibly fewer flowers at the base to fill in the gap.

• Here I selected a wispy organdy ribbon that could float with any passing breeze on a hot summer's day. Save heavy silks, satins, and velvets for cooler weather.

Aren't We a Pair?

Repetition is a powerful element in design. I once spied a display window on Madison Avenue in New York where the only decoration among the fashions were brown paper bags, standing open on the floor of the display. There were many of them. One would have looked silly, but thirty were eye stopping. Years later I have no memory of the clothing they were meant to highlight, only the elegance of those bags marching across the space.

Two small topiaries are more than twice as compelling as one. Two form an instant centerpiece on a dining room table, placed two feet away from each other. Two can bracket precious objects on a shelf. Two can stand sentinel among a group of framed photos. Just imagine how three would look in a larger space.

From the construction point of view, not only does the pair take more time and materials, it's extremely hard to get them to look identical, so I'm tolerant of differences. Working with natural plant materials means accepting variation in hue, tint, and size. Even using the same vine to construct both wreath bases, one can have more twig offshoots than the other. Rather than force the issue of conformity by snipping off the twigs, I am happy with the concept of "the same but different." To balance the two, I may add one small branch to the base of one topiary, shown on p. 38.

WHAT YOU NEED (FOR EACH)

assorted dried flowers, leaves, pods, and berries, such as roses, peonies, globe amaranth, strawflowers, pink pepper berries, love-in-a-mist, and baker fern

vine wreath base, 7" in diameter, or 1–1½ yards vine to make your own

stick, 10" long and ¾" in diameter

ruler

paring knife

glue gun and glue sticks

floral shears

container, approximately 6" high and 4–5" in diameter

1 block floral foam for dried flowers (usually brown)

green sheet moss or 1 handful Spanish moss (optional)

18" narrow ribbon (optional)

Beyond the Garden

WHAT YOU DO

1. Purchase or make a vine wreath base by wrapping some fresh vine around itself, weaving it in and out until it holds together and is as thick as you want it. If the vine isn't fresh cut, soak it in hot water for at least twelve hours or overnight to make the wood pliable enough to wrap.

2. Measure and cut the stick eight to ten inches long, cutting it into points at both ends.

3. Slip one end through the woven vine to make a "lollipop" and secure it in place with a glob of glue.

4. Cut foam to just fit the container and insert.

5. Glue flowers and leaves on the wreath base, either on one face or two, depending on where you will showcase this topiary. If you plan a pair for the dining room table, by all means decorate both sides of each.

6. When you are satisfied with the arrangement, stick the whole topiary firmly into the foam. You only get one shot at this. If you change your mind on the placement and take the stick out to reinsert it, you must use a new piece of foam, lest the topiary be too wobbly.

7. Cover the foam with the moss or any other material you have a lot of, such as the pepper berries here. Then glue a few more flowers and leaves at the base around the "trunk."

8. If you choose to add ribbon, make a bow at the top of the trunk, just under the wreath base.

Topiaries

Beyond the Garden

If you are making a pair of topiaries, starting with wreaths the same size will give you the best chance for identical twins. Continue to work on both simultaneously rather than one at a time. Glue leaves on one, then the other. Add the first type of flower on each, then the second type of flower, and so forth. Working simultaneously also guards against running out of materials halfway through the second topiary.

If you're gluing flowers on one side only as shown here, I find it best to decorate the topiary and then insert it into the foam rather than working in the reverse order. Once the stem is inserted, you don't want to loosen it by knocking against it. If you are decorating both sides with flowers, you can insert the stem after decorating one side, being careful as you work on the second side. Or take the precaution of standing the topiary in a spare piece of foam while you work on it, then transfer it to the container at the end.

Topiaries

Frame-Ups

*You may break, you may shatter the vase if you will
but the scent of the roses will hang round it still.*

— Thomas Moore, Irish Melodies

Hang on a wall, stand on a mantelpiece, or prop on a table: dried flower collages serve multiple purposes. Sometimes the flowers form the frame, highlighting and decorating the precious photos within. Sometimes the flowers *are* the picture and the frame is incidental. When you design collages with keepsake flowers, you create both decoration and memento of a special event. A framed piece without the glass will allow the aroma to "hang round it still."

Chapter 4

You're Invited

A special invitation or announcement in the mail signals pleasurable anticipation and often the need for a gift. Whether wedding, baby shower, anniversary, graduation party, Bat Mitzvah, or christening, a personalized gift is appreciated. The framed announcement or invitation returned with dried keepsake flowers is unlikely to be duplicated.

In advance I request permission from the honoree (or her mother) to take home some flowers from the event. Perhaps a centerpiece, flowers from the altar, or other floral bouquet. It needn't be an armload.

Keep flowers fresh and initiate the drying process as soon after the event as possible. Many times have I dashed through airports to fly home from a wedding with an arrangement of fresh flowers in wet floral foam. People smile and make way. The flight attendants give me extra help with the overhead compartment, and someone invariably offers to accept the flowers as a gift. In fact, traveling with fresh flowers attracts even more smiles than traveling with a baby or a dog, as they're not known to cry or bark.

If you've only managed to garner a few keepsake flowers or if you've had to pass up the event completely, use some substitutes from your own stock.

Beyond the Garden

WHAT YOU NEED

white larkspur

ivy and rose leaves

roses

invitation or announcement

scissors

shadow box frame, 2–3" deep

white craft glue

ruler

glue gun and glue sticks (optional)

WHAT YOU DO

1   Start the flowers drying. Either air-dry, press, or dry in silica gel. Here the roses were dried in silica gel, the ivy leaves were pressed, and the white larkspur was air-dried by hanging. All three processes are described on pp.121–126.

2   The flowers will take two to three weeks to dry completely. During that time purchase a shadow box frame, at least two inches but preferably three inches in depth, depending on the size of the flowers. If your local frame shop doesn't have one, try one of the frame catalogs such as *Exposures* (www.exposures online.com; 1-800-222-4947). The mat should be archival paper or fabric (also called museum board or acid-free board).

3   Examine the invitation or announcement. That is the focal point of the design. The flowers will decorate and highlight it. Use the invitation whole or cut it to show the most decorative parts. In this example, the bride selected the wedding invitation for the painting on the front. I wanted to show much of the painting, but overlapped it with the printed information inside. Each invitation poses a separate design challenge.

4   When the flowers are dried and ready, assemble all your materials. Open the back of the shadow box and work on the mat. Position the invitation and the flowers first to try different designs before you glue.

5   Use white glue to secure the invitation, measuring so you have even borders.

6   Glue the flowers on with the glue gun (or use additional white glue for this), starting with the largest roses. Then add some leaves, then the smaller roses. Tuck in some pieces of larkspur or other spiked flowers, trimming as necessary to fit. End with extra leaves.

7   Give the white glue a day or so to dry. Sign discreetly with your initials in the corner, if desired, and put the mat back in the frame. Gift wrap for presentation.

TIP:
Some invitations are printed on single-faced cardstock; others are double folded. If the invitation is particularly decorative on the front, request a second invitation from a family member or friend who also received one so you have an extra to cut up and include in the collage.

TIP:
If using only one face of a traditional-style engraved invitation, plan two L-shaped designs of flowers on two opposite corners: a larger L of flowers in the bottom left and a smaller L at the top right, abutting the edge of the paper. They balance nicely and highlight the printing in grand style.

Frame-Ups

Keepsake Flowers

Many of the most beautiful wedding bouquets contain flowers that are impossible to preserve just by hanging: lilies, orchids, lilacs, and tulips, for example. While an all-rose bouquet can be quickly disassembled, air-dried by hanging, and reassembled in a smaller version of its former self, other bouquets need more precise handling.

In addition to weddings, other important occasions also generate keepsake flowers that are precious to the recipient: a Valentine's bouquet sent by the love of one's life, even funeral flowers of a beloved family member.

Here is an example of a keepsake designed from a wedding bouquet featuring lilies, roses, and lilacs.

WHAT YOU NEED

wedding bouquet or other keepsake flowers

floral shears

silica gel, sand, kitty litter, or your favorite drying medium

dust mask/respirator if using silica gel

shadow box frame with acid-free mat or material, 2–3" deep (this one is 11" x 14")

pencil

glue gun and glue sticks

WHAT YOU DO

1   Prepare the flowers for immersing in the silica gel, sand, or other desiccant by cutting all the stems as short as possible. Remove stamens from the lilies; the pollen from the stamens will stain the picture. This is always done by florists, but sometimes new buds will open between the time the bouquet leaves the shop and the time you get to work. Dry the flowers in the silica following instructions on pp. 125–126. Be sure to wear a dust mask during this step.

2   Press rose leaves (not petals), if included, following instructions on pp. 123–125.

3   Assemble all the materials after the flowers have dried; it usually takes about three weeks.

4   Open the shadow box and work on the mat. Often you have lots of flowers and must organize them in some way rather than just scattering them at random.

Plan a shape for the design. A favorite of many flower designers is a reverse S shape, here turned on its side.

5   Lightly draw the S or another shape on the mat with the pencil.

6   Place the flowers in position along the S, starting with the largest first, here the lilies and large roses. Continue with the smaller roses, then the lilacs. Tuck in the leaves.

7   When you are satisfied, start gluing the flowers in place until all are secure. If you have more flowers than you can possibly cram into the design, save them for potpourri rather than lose the shape of the design.

8   Before replacing the back of the shadow box, turn the whole thing over and gently tap the mat to shake out any crumbs.

9   Hang the picture out of direct sunlight to preserve the colors for as long as possible.

Beyond the Garden

Quilting Bee

The craft of quilting inspires this design. I've always admired both contemporary and traditional quilt patterns, but I can't seem to find the time or patience to produce those neat and tiny stitches. Granted, this rose quilt won't keep you warm in winter, but many quilts are now displayed as art pieces, and you can do the same with this. Exhibit it on the wall, on a mantel, or propped in a stand on a side table. The possible patterns are infinite, both for the individual squares and for positioning them within a frame.

Designing the rose quilt demands planning ahead. Select a shadow box frame with glass or a shallower frame without glass. Choose a square or rectangle, or have one made to your dimensions at a frame shop. Order one to your specifications, getting the color, size, and style you need for a particular project. For a wedding gift, suit the colors to the preferences of the couple. The cost is not much above a ready-made frame unless you choose something elaborate. Take time to select a pleasing mat color as you may elect to have some of the mat visible as part of the design.

The amount of materials needed will of course depend on the size of the frame and how many squares you are making.

WHAT YOU NEED

roses, rose leaves, or other flowers and herbs in varying colors and shapes (see tip below)

silica gel

airtight container

dust mask/respirator

scissors or floral shears

flower press or heavy phone books

square or rectangular shadow box frame

acid-free mat board, also called museum board

ruler

pencil

glue gun and glue sticks

art gum eraser

WHAT YOU DO

1 Dry the flowers first, or purchase air-dried or freeze-dried roses or pressed flowers.

2 You may air-dry the roses by hanging them in small bunches in a warm, dark, dry place. But to attain a more perfect look, dry them in silica gel. To dry the roses in silica gel, wear a dust mask/respirator. Pour a one-inch layer of silica gel in the bottom of an airtight container.

3 Snip off the stems of the roses completely, leaving only the swelling at the base of the flower. Snip off the leaves and set aside (see step 6).

4 Stand each rose upright in the silica gel, close to the others but not touching.

5 Pour the remaining silica gel gently around the flowers, building it up until they are completely buried under another inch of the sandy gel. Cover the container.

Leave undisturbed for three weeks, then pour off the silica gel and save to reuse. I've used mine for fourteen years, hence the little flecks of past projects that are visible in the sand. Shake all the silica off the roses and set them aside. (See pp. 125–126 for more details.)

6 Meanwhile, press the leaves that came off the roses in a flower press or heavy phone book. When the flowers are ready, the leaves will also be ready. (For more information, see pp. 123–125.)

7 To prepare the frame, measure the mat and block it into squares with light pencil marks. Here the measurement of the mat is fifteen and a half by fifteen and a half inches. I left one-quarter inch of mat around the edge; it will be hidden under the frame. The finished size of the quilt is fifteen by fifteen inches, divided into nine five-by-five-inch squares.

Beyond the Garden

8   Visualize the placement of your flowers and leaves. Plan ahead. Then place your materials where you think they should go without gluing them down. Make any necessary changes at this point. Then glue the flowers and leaves in place.

9   Remove any visible pencil marks with the eraser.

TIP:

This quilt, designed only with roses and rose leaves, looks equally spectacular with other dried flowers and herbs from your garden or a floral shop. As with sewn quilts, your design is limited only by your imagination and your materials. Give your quilt another name or a theme and you'll immediately know what you need. For a patriotic quilt use red cockscomb and roses; white strawflowers, pearly everlasting, feverfew, or money plant (*Lunaria*); and blue globe thistle, delphinium, bachelor's button, or statice.

To complement modern decor, opt for hot colors: the golds of perennial sunflower (*Heliopsis)* and yarrow, bright purples and hot pinks of statice and globe amaranth, reds of cockscomb and small dried hot peppers.

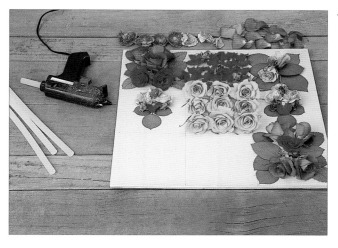

TIP:

Dried flowers hold their color best if they are displayed away from direct sunlight in an environment with low humidity. For example, avoid a bathroom that gets a lot of steam and any location near a window. Sealing the finished quilt under glass in a shadow box will also help preserve the colors. But the best tip of all is to start with strong colors as I have here. No wimpy pastel pinks, no pale yellows, no creams. The orange red of 'Mercedes' or 'Tropicana' roses are very long lasting.

Framing the Past

Sorting through old photographs is a task for a long, rainy afternoon.

Treasures are to be found in the frayed carton where they have been shoved and stored for decades. Perhaps the photos were given to you after an older generation could no longer house the family archives. The tones of black, white, and sepia; the period dress and coiffures; even the stances of the subjects suggest other worlds. Fathers and sons, brothers and their wives now take up residence in your home where you decide to display some of your favorites.

Frames are to be found not only in your own attic but also at every yard sale, flea market, and thrift shop around the country. Many have a damaged finish or are downright ugly. Covering the surface with dried flowers enhances the period feel of the photos while covering the sins of the old frame.

Frame the future as well as the past. Create a rosy gift especially appropriate for a baby, engagement, or bridal shower. Personalized frames are always appreciated at these times of happy anticipation.

In selecting a frame for this process, choose wood or fabric-covered; both readily accept the hot glue, whereas metal and glass frames won't. Also look for a frame that is at least an inch wide, enough surface to allow you to afix the flowers.

Beyond the Garden

WHAT YOU NEED

assorted dried materials:

for a large frame, 1 head dried blue hydrangea, a handful of roses, and 6–12 leaves

for a small frame, 8–12 stems dried horsetail and a handful of roses

picture frame, old and ugly will do just fine

black spray paint (optional)

scissors or floral shears

glue gun and glue sticks

ruler (optional)

WHAT YOU DO

1   Clean the frame and glass as needed. Remove the glass and spray the frame with black paint to hide any unwanted colors peeking through, if desired. Without the paint you will have to be a little more careful in placing the flowers.

2   Put your picture in the frame and reassemble with glass and backing. Do this now, as it is hard to work once the flowers are in position. If giving as a gift, put a piece of clean mat board inside in frame.

3   For a large frame, cut a head of blue hydrangea into smaller clusters. Glue them all around the frame. One large hydrangea was enough for this whole frame. Then glue on the leaves anywhere it is sparse. Finish with the roses, scattered throughout the hydrangea.

4   For a small frame, measure and cut stems of dried horsetail (*Equisetum hyemale*) or other thick grass to cover the frame. Glue in place, working one side at a time. Add the roses.

TIP:

Plan ahead to distribute both hydrangea and roses evenly. There are many systems to do this, and I'm sure you'll find your own, whether counting and sorting or laying the flowers on first without glue before gluing in place. Another favorite method is to work on all four sides at once, filling in as you go until you run out of flowers. When you get very experienced with flower crafts—whether creating frames, wreaths, or arrangements—your eye makes automatic adjustments to take care of all sides. Yet I never expect my work to be perfectly even, as natural materials vary. Even the horsetail, which seems almost identical from one stem to the next, really isn't. They get narrower toward the top, and no two stems are exactly alike.

Frame-Ups

Floral Loom

Remember as a child weaving pot holders on a small loom? You gave them to Mother, Grandma, and your favorite aunts, until there was no cook left without a colorful gift and the loom got buried under newer toys in the back of your closet.

This project is just as easy as those long-ago pot holders and just as much fun to do. It uses the same simple weaving technique, only with long- and short-stemmed herbs and flowers on a loom you make yourself.

Here I chose a color combination of blues and yellows. The gold frame and gold cords are all part of the scheme. It's not easy to find true blue, rather than lavender, in flowers. Try statice, globe thistle, delphinium, or sea holly (*Eryngium*) for natural blues. See another finished project on p. 128.

WHAT YOU NEED

an assortment of dried flowers and herbs, here 10 stems goldenrod, 5 stems pitcher plant (*Saracenia*)*, 5 stems delphinium, 7–10 stems sea holly, 8–10 pieces tansy, 10 pieces Australian daisy, and 16 roses

picture frame with the glass, wire, and mat removed and discarded (this one measures 12" x 16" in the interior)

9 yards cord or very narrow ribbon

scissors or floral shears

flat picture hanger with two tiny brads

glue gun and glue sticks (optional)

* Pitcher plant is a protected flower in some locals. My material comes from a wholesale source, which assures me that the herbs and flowers are grown for resale.

Beyond the Garden

WHAT YOU DO

1. Tie the cord to one corner of the frame and wrap it around the frame the long way, leaving about two inches between strands. Here I have six strands to form the warp of the loom. The flowers and herbs are the weft.

2. Cut the cord and tie tightly to the opposite corner. Use your fingers to even out the spaces between the cord.

3. Decide which way you want your weaving to hang. Nail the picture hanger to the back of the frame now, when you won't be damaging a lot of dried materials.

4. Take the stem end of one piece of goldenrod or other herb such as 'Silver King' artemisia and position it along the short side of the frame. Don't measure and cut the herbs in advance because you'll use a little more than the edge-to-edge measurement in the weaving process. Weave under and over each of the six strands on the top layer. Ignore the strands wrapping in the back. Pull until the tip of the flowers reaches the inner edge of the frame.

5. Trim off any extra stem now or wait until later and trim all the stems at once.

6. Take the next stem and start weaving from the other side. Remember that if the previous stem ended with an "over," start with an "under."

7. Keep alternating until you have a base that is not too tightly packed. In this design I used fresh goldenrod, because I know it will dry in place and I had it on hand at the time. The pitcher plant would also dry in place, but I didn't have the fresh version.

8. What you weave next is a matter of taste, how much you have of each variety, and how long the stems are. I always save the roses for last because I want them to show. The delphinium will come next to last because I crave that blue color.

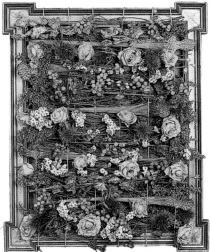

9. Toward the end, survey your weaving. As the loom gets full, it is much harder to pull stems all the way through without damaging other material. Now there is no need. The loom is full enough. You can cut a stem short and tuck it under one strand of cord and it will stay in place. If all else fails, there's always the glue gun, but purists will want to keep strictly to weaving on this project.

10. Do a last trimming of stem ends near the frame to tidy up the picture.

11. Hang vertically or horizontally, whichever fits your space best.

TIP: SELECTING A FRAME

If the frame is attractive as is this one, I like to have it showing, cutting the stems to fit the inside of the frame. If the frame is ugly, spray paint it black to cover, then cut the stems to reach to the outer edge. The frame will thus support the flowers and herbs but will be largely invisible. Select a frame of a moderate size that can accommodate the length of common flowers. If you want a bigger weaving, you'll have to use two or more stems to reach across the frame.

TIP: SELECTING MATERIAL

In addition to color, which is often a prime consideration, observe the appearance of the flower. Some, like goldenrod and artemisia, are bushy and have leaves or flowers that fan out. Others, like larkspur, delphinium, pitcher plant, and gay feather (*Liatris*), have small flowers growing eight to twelve inches along the stem. Still others, like roses, statice, sea holly, or globe thistle, have the interest mainly at the top. I usually try to find some of each of these types for a weaving.

Frame Ups

Trying to ImPress

It's not necessary to press huge quantities of flowers in order to make a beautiful picture.

Here are two ideas using minimal amounts of pressed materials but handling them in interesting ways. Instructions for pressing appear on pp. 123–125. One stem of delphinium and two roses are all that's needed to make an abstract design. It helps that the frame and mat are both old and interesting. Scouring flea markets and antique shops for frames is part of the fun.

Beyond the Garden

WHAT YOU NEED

1 stem delphinium

2 roses

flower press and absorbent paper

tweezers

acid-free mat board

ruler

pencil

X-acto knife

white glue that dries clear

toothpicks

frame and top mat (purchase with the frame or have one
    professionally cut)

WHAT YOU DO

1   Remove the delphinium flowers from the stem and
    position them in the press face down.

2   Gently remove the petals from the roses and position
    them on a separate page in the press, leaving at least
    one-quarter inch between petals.

3   Tighten the press and follow directions for pressing on
    pp. 123–125.

4   When the whole flowers and petals are dry and ready
    (in about three weeks), open the press and remove
    them using the tweezers if necessary to pick them up.

5   Meanwhile prepare the frame. Measure the acid-free
    mat board and cut it to fit the frame with the X-acto
    knife. It's nice to have a top mat as well. Lightly trace
    the opening of the top mat onto the bottom mat with
    the pencil. Now you know where to glue the flowers.

6   Start at the top of the acid-free mat board. Using a
    toothpick, dab the glue in two tiny spots onto a rose
    petal, then place it on the mat using the tweezers.
    Press with your hand. Make an overlapping row with
    rose petals. Continue making more rows.

7   About two-thirds of the way down (not in the middle
    of the mat), add a row of delphinium flowers, then add
    more rows of flowers and petals until you reach the
    bottom.

8   Put the top mat on top and check that all spaces are
    covered. Let it dry for two days. Now assemble the
    picture in the frame with the glass.

9   Hang the picture out of direct sunlight for the longest-
    lasting color.

Frame-Ups

VARIATIONS ON A THEME

Old botanical prints are the inspiration for this picture. Botanicals usually depict the whole flower, as well as the bud, leaves, sepals, stamens, and other parts of the plant, including the fruit and sometimes the roots.

Here I used an old rose print and had a framer cut a mat with two openings, one for the print and one for my few pressed pieces. I bought the frame, mat, and glass complete but unassembled. This allowed me to add my pressed flowers, then put it all together myself or take it back to the framer to assemble. The rose I selected is small, making it simple to press whole. There isn't much danger of mildew in a flower of this size. It's only the bigger, thicker roses that threaten to go moldy in the press. Press whole roses on one page and leaves, sepals, and other very thin parts on another. Buds need their own page as well, as their thickness is intermediary. Follow the instructions for pressing on pp. 123–125 and the instructions for gluing in step 6 on p. 53. Parts of the plant are scattered in a pleasing balance, each piece displaying its true nature.

Frame-Ups

Seasonal Delights

O my Luve's like a red, red rose,
That's newly sprung in June;
O my luve's like the melodie,
That's sweetly played in tune.

— Robert Burns

Whether from the garden or the florist, roses can be arranged formally or informally once they cross your threshold. Appearance depends on the container, the style of design, the site, and the accompanying materials. Pairing roses with fruits and vegetables is a welcome innovation, often a complete surprise to the viewer, who reacts with delight. The color of the roses and the season of the year determine the fruit or vegetable. Fruits and vegetables can be arranged in the container with the roses or piled up by themselves in a beautiful still life.

Here are five designs that aim to capture the glory of the season with fresh or dried roses.

Lemonade

A refreshing pitcher of "lemonade" in a rose arbor is a harbinger of summer. The lemons serve two functions: an artistic one, contributing their bright color to the monochromatic arrangement, and a mechanical one, holding the stems in place.

Beyond the Garden

A monochromatic theme makes flower decisions easy. Cut whatever yellow roses you might have or buy a few in different shades of yellow, then add foliage and other flowers in the same color range. Spring always brings an exciting selection of yellows in the garden, such as hosta leaves, lady's mantle, and yarrow.

The fruit supplants the need for metal frogs, glass marbles, tape, or chicken wire, any of which are typically used in clear containers to hold flowers in place.

WHAT YOU NEED

3 small hosta leaves

5 stems yellow forsythia leaves

9 hakonechloa fronds (grass)

9 stems lady's mantle

15 roses, here a combination of 'Timeless,' 'Autumn Sunset,' 'Sun Flare,' and 'Yellow Meidiland'

7 yarrow

8 or more unblemished lemons

crystal or glass pitcher or vase

water mixed with floral preservative

floral shears

plastic lazy Susan (optional)

WHAT YOU DO

1 Wash lemons and arrange them in the pitcher according to its size and shape. This pitcher is eight inches tall and six inches wide at the top, with a nice bulge in the middle. It was a perfect fit for eight lemons.

2 Add water to the pitcher almost to the top of the lemons. If you add too much they will start to float.

3 Cut the stems of foliage (hosta, forsythia, and hakonechloa) eight to ten inches in length. Place them at the edges of the pitcher. Add the lady's mantle.

4 Insert the roses, cutting the stems as short as you need. They just have to nestle between the lemons to be held in place and need not reach all the way to the bottom of the arrangement. Walk around the arrangement for even placement, or use a lazy Susan under the pitcher.

5 Fill in the arrangement with the other flowers. Since this arrangement highlights the four varieties of roses that I had available, not much more is necessary.

6 Add fresh water every day or so to prolong the life of the flowers. The lemons will probably last longer than the arrangement and are still edible after the flowers and foliage are consigned to the compost heap.

Beyond the Garden

VARIATIONS ON A THEME:
APPLE PUNCH

Other citrus fruits such as limes and small oranges also work beautifully, changing the nature of the design with their assertive color. For the fall, select apples, hard pears, crab apples, or unblemished cranberries, all of which last for weeks. Select floral materials appropriate to the season and to the fruit. For Christmas, apples or cranberries are perfect with evergreen boughs and holly berries. Be sure to wash and pick over the fruit to remove soft and blemished pieces, then place the fruit in the container first before adding the water, so it doesn't float.

This is a fall holiday arrangement made in a punch bowl. The colors cast a warm and wonderful glow on the festive table. While many of the flowers are from the florist, the clerodendron berries, some of the mums, and the rose hips are the last cuttings from my own garden.

Summer Still Life

Transform two unrelated crystal pieces into a set for a summer still life. Nothing proclaims the season like fruit from a local orchard. This cylindrical "vase" is actually a wine cooler that nestles comfortably inside the fruit bowl. You could as easily use a real cylindrical vase, which may be more readily available. Once you assemble this pair, the rest falls neatly into place. Start with fruit that is very firm and flowers that are very fresh. You need only a minimal number of roses for this contemporary style because they are completely encapsulated and need some breathing room when they open fully.

WHAT YOU NEED

5 roses

floral preservative

crystal or glass fruit bowl and cylindrical vase

glass marbles

floral shears

nectarines, Queen Anne cherries, and small yellow plums

WHAT YOU DO

1   Condition the flowers well (see pp. 118–120) so they absorb maximum water before placing them in the vase.

2   Place the marbles in the bottom of the vase; you'll need a layer about three inches deep. Add approximately four inches of water.

3   Cut the stems of the roses short, so the heads will stand beneath the rim of the vase. Stand them carefully around the perimeter of the vase with their tops even. Fill in the center of the vase with additional roses.

4   Add the nectarines, cherries, and plums to the bowl. Replace them as they are eaten and replace the water in the vase as it is absorbed.

VARIATIONS ON A THEME

Pair bright-red roses with small plums and red cherries using the same design. Because these roses have smaller flowers, I used ten instead of five.

TIP:

The gap between the cylinder and the edge of the fruit bowl was only one and three-quarter inches, that's why I selected all small pieces of fruit. If you're using a wider bowl such as a punch bowl, you can select larger fruit, such as peaches or apples.

Autumn Still Life

The roses blush from cream to crimson and are accompanied by a few stems of burgundy foliage from the flowering plum tree. An old orange watering can holds two dozen roses easily. Rather than place the arrangement in the house, it sits on a bench by the front door of my old Pennsylvania farmhouse, welcoming all comers. I probably enjoy it more than anyone else, taking quiet pleasure in the design each time I enter and leave.

The rest of the materials are gathered from the field, a farm stand, and in the case of the green osage oranges, the roadside. I may have been spotted on Red Dale Road on my hands and knees, rescuing the fallen fruit from being crushed by the few cars that pass by.

An assortment of pumpkins, squash, peppers, and autumn leaves are piled rather haphazardly around the watering can. Apples and pears would also speak of the fall harvest and could replace any of the other elements. Look for fruit that are firm and unblemished, as these will last longest.

TIP: Place this arrangement where it is shaded during the day and where it can enjoy the cool autumn temperatures at night. If you expect a sudden overnight frost, bring in the watering can, replacing it among the other materials in the morning.

VARIATIONS ON A THEME

For another type of celebration, with or without the flowers, concentrate on peppers, both sweet and hot, in tropical colors such as red, yellow, and orange.

Here the materials include lemons and artichokes along with bell peppers, hot Thai peppers, a few small apples, and squash saved from the garden. Dried pink pepper berries stand in lieu of the grapes, filling in corners and drooping gracefully.

HOW LONG WILL IT LAST?

With fruits, vegetables, and flowers, the answer is, "It depends." The arrangement will have the longest life if you:

• Select the items carefully. Choose roses just coming into bloom, rather than those already fully open or starting to fade. Select plums and other fruit that are firm with no blemishes.

• Items should be dry when you paint them with egg white or glue.

• The cooler and less humid the room, the longer the arrangement will last. For a garden party, this and all other food will do better in the shade.

I used the pepper arrangement to decorate my farmhouse for a tour to benefit the local library. After the house tour, during which the arrangement was greatly admired, I put the whole tray outdoors on a bench under cover by my front door. The arrangement looked wonderful for another two weeks in the frigid December air, undamaged by the frequent early morning frosts.

A NOTE ON SAFETY

In the olden days we blithely accepted uncooked egg whites in certain recipes. Whites were used on occasion to crystallize fruits and flowers that were then considered to be edible decorations. Crystallized violets and rose petals decorated platters of cookies and petit fours and could be savored with tea.

Now we know that raw eggs might harbor harmful bacteria. Even though the dried egg whites I used to make the sugar plums have been pasteurized, therefore are probably edible when fresh, I think it's best to keep this as an "eyes-only" design. The tray of peppers was made with the white glue and is certainly "eyes only."

TIP:
Regular table sugar works in the same way but is not nearly as pretty as coarse sugar, which has larger crystals. Coarse sugar is available in light brown as well, but for fruits and flowers white is best.

Hi-Ho Silver

If you've grown 'Silver King' artemisia you know it always rewards the gardener with a big, bushy display. Of course the display is muted gray, but it's fragrant and has an interesting texture, with tiny balls of bloom along the stem. The plant is excellent for xeriscaping where drought may be a problem, and it's reliable year after year. You can use the foliage in fresh arrangements or hang to air-dry, but there's always too much.

Make yourself an artemisia basket with two rubber bands and some ribbon. Then add whatever dried flowers the late summer brings you. This basket-making technique is for those of us who wouldn't dream of attempting an intricate reed affair.

WHAT YOU NEED

1 big bunch (20–25 stems) of tall dried artemisia

assorted dried flowers, here 24 roses, 15–20 globe amaranth, 12–15 stems yarrow, 12–15 stems amaranth, 7–10 stems goldenrod

ruler

scissors and floral shears

2 large rubber bands

2½ yards narrow ribbon or raffia

WHAT YOU DO

Making the Basket

1 Select four well-branched, tall stems of artemisia. Set aside.

2 Cut the rest of the artemisia into six-inch lengths, measuring from the tips. Each stem will probably give you at least two pieces.

3 Make a big, even pile of the pieces. Wrap the rubber bands around the pile, about one and one half inches from the top and one and one half inches from the bottom.

4 You now have a nice artemisia log. Stand it up. Trim the bottom carefully if it doesn't stand evenly.

5 Cut the ribbon into two one-yard pieces and one half-yard piece. If using raffia, grab a half-handful of strands for each tie.

6 Slip two of the reserved tall stems on one side under the rubber bands, and the other two reserved stems on the opposite side. Grab the top of the stems, one pair in each hand, and slowly bring them toward the middle and cross. Check the look before you tie them together with the half-yard piece of ribbon. You may want to trim the stem end to make the handle shorter before you proceed.

7 Tie the two one-yard pieces of ribbon over the rubber bands to hide them, making small bows. Trim ribbon as desired. I always start with more ribbon than I need since I prefer to decide how big a bow I want after I see the finished design.

Making the Arrangement

1 Since it's autumn and I have beautiful flame-colored dried roses, the fall fields are my inspiration. I find red amaranth, goldenrod, orange globe amaranth, and wild white yarrow to accompany them.

2 Start with the red amaranth, cut the stems short and insert them in the basket. They will stay in place without any other mechanics. If you don't have amaranth, start with any flower or grass that will droop over the sides of the basket.

Beyond the Garden

3 Add the goldenrod and yarrow, turning the basket to make the placement as even as possible. Cut the stems as needed so they don't hide the handle. Then add the major color jolt, the globe amaranth, ending with the roses that have been steamed open (see p. 129 for instructions).

Uh-oh! The goldenrod, which I thought was perfectly placed, now sticks out and detracts from the finished design in several spots. If I try to pull it out, lots of other flowers will be ruined. I take my trusty floral shears and give it a small haircut. Just like the best stylist, I find a few snips make all the difference.

I add as well as subtract. The tips of the handle above the cross look uneven, so I stick in a few small pieces to even it up. No one will ever know.

VARIATIONS ON A THEME
Follow the same basketmaking instructions substituting other materials. Each will give a very different look. I've used wild goldenrod, which is available in abundance in the Northeast, and I've used gay feather, which is stiffer, but provides a beautiful color. Instead of bending and crossing the stems for the handle, I left the side pieces vertical and tied the ribbon onto two horizontal pieces as a crossbar.

These baskets are beautiful enough to be viewed on their own, but flowers add even more interest.

Fragrance and Taste

I know a bank whereon the wild thyme blows,
Where oxlips and the nodding violet grows
Quite over-canopied with luscious woodbine
With sweet musk-roses and with eglantine*

—William Shakespeare,
A Midsummer Night's Dream

*An old garden species of shrub rose.

Chapter 6

Potpourri

A potpourri is a stew, mixture, medley, or collection and most commonly refers to a glorious mixture of botanicals that scent the home and please the eye.

In the commercial marketplace there is a huge variation in quality, aesthetics, and prices of potpourris. Dyed wood shavings replace dried flowers and herbs to bring down the cost. Artificial scents add a harsh or cloying note to the aroma. Although rose petals are used in many commercial potpourris as part of the mixture, their delicate scent is often overpowered by manufactured fragrances.

When I take the time and make the effort to bake, I use butter, never margarine or vegetable shortening, to produce the most flavorful results. My theory is to make every calorie count. So it is with potpourris. The finest ingredients produce fabulous results.

Beyond the Garden

When you make your own potpourris you have the agreeable task of combining many delightful ingredients; the very act of mixing the "stew" gives pleasure. Some prefer to combine all the ingredients, then dole out the mixtures into bowls and packages for gift giving, adding one or two special flowers on the top. Others prefer to arrange their potpourris meticulously in layers and rows. Either way you will have a personalized product.

Dried potpourris are most common, but moist potpourris were popular in past centuries and were sometimes called "sweet jars." Fresh or dried rose petals and other scented flowers and herbs were layered with spices, oils, and uniodized salt and left to ferment for several weeks, being compressed with weights or stirred daily. Moist potpourris are more work and are unattractive in appearance. They are typically stored in a porcelain jar with a perforated, tightly fitting lid. The perforations allow the aroma to waft into the room while hiding the brown mush inside.

There are four basic considerations for any potpourri: aroma, texture, color, and longevity. Aroma is an absolute necessity; the others are not. You can keep the mixture in a lidded porcelain jar with holes to let the scent escape while hiding the contents, so texture and color become irrelevant. You can stir and bruise the potpourri weekly to release additional scent, add a few drops of essential oils as the original scent begins to fade, or make a new mixture every year. Mixing a new potpourri is a treat. So longevity becomes a nonissue.

The longevity of potpourris and dried flowers and herbs in general has been vastly exaggerated by commercial interests. Any arrangement or mixture should be tossed on the compost pile after a maximum of two years, if only to get rid of the accumulation of dust.

Aroma

Favorite scents are both universal and highly individualistic, based on both biology and experience. Special scents from childhood that evoke pleasant memories are particularly powerful. A whiff of summer phlox never fails to stimulate a memory of myself at three years old with a favorite uncle in a summer garden. I plant calendula and tomatoes some years just so I can smell the leaves and recall more early memories.

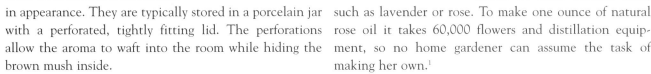

Sometimes I use natural essential oils to contribute most or all of the fragrance and concentrate on color and texture in the recipe. Essential oils, which you can purchase in small, dark-glass vials with droppers, provide scents that aren't readily available, such as patchouli or sandalwood. Oils enhance the fragrance of ingredients in their natural form, such as lavender or rose. To make one ounce of natural rose oil it takes 60,000 flowers and distillation equipment, so no home gardener can assume the task of making her own.[1]

Old-fashioned roses add a sweet fragrance, as do rose geranium leaves, lavender, lemon verbena, mountain mint, sweet Annie, heliotrope, lily of the valley, peony, and gardenia. Beware of modern varieties such as some hybrid roses where aroma has been sacrificed for other desirable qualities such as bloom size and color. Use rosebuds or petals for their looks, but the strongest fragrance emanates from the whole, opened dried flower.

For pungent and spicy smells try bergamot, pinks and carnations, cloves, nutmeg, cinnamon, eucalyptus, orange, lemon and grapefruit rind, curry plant, tansy, yarrow, sage, juniper, spruce and other conifer needles, star anise, patchouli, and sandalwood.

[1]Lesley Bremness, Herbs, (London: DK Ltd., 1994), 22.

Fragrance and Taste

Texture

Add texture to your potpourri by using some choice botanicals that have little or no scent but are interesting to look at and touch; they will make a nice contrast to the more delicate dried blossoms and petals. Using a few whole flowers in mixtures that consist of mostly broken pieces and petals contributes immensely to visual appeal. Try air-dried roses on top of a potpourri of rose petals or dried Queen Anne's lace atop any floral or woodsy combination.

Some excellent botanicals for texture are small conifer cones such as hemlock, small flower pods such as love-in-a-mist and Oriental nigella, globe thistle, rose hips, pussy willow catkins, juniper and other dried berries, Kentucky coffee beans, Job's tears or other large seeds, small clusters of hydrangea flowers, leaves and buds of lamb's ears, and any whole dried flower with an interesting shape.

Color

Many cheap mixtures combine colors indiscriminately, but the most beautiful potpourris are often those that maintain a particular color palette, blending tones in one color range. With roses the most obvious range is pink to red, or all pastels, but flame orange to gold and pale yellow is unexpected and beautiful. Add dried calendula, pompon dahlias, marigolds, or perennial sunflowers to extend the sunshine theme.

Also try designing with opposite colors on the color wheel. Try yellow and purple, orange and blue, or red and green. Make a fabulous winter potpourri of dried red roses and green conifer needles, with a few small cones thrown in for texture and some spicy scents like clove to meld with the sweet rose.

Longevity

Most potpourri recipes call for a fixative to keep the aromas from dissipating too quickly. The fixatives often contribute a fragrance of their own, thus adding a second value to the mixture. One of the fixatives most commonly used is orrisroot, the root of the Florentine iris, dried and finely chopped or ground into a powder. If you can't find it anywhere else, ask a pharmacist to order it for you. The chopped form is better to use for potpourri than the powder, as powdered orrisroot as well as cinnamon, another fixative, will coat the ingredients with a light film, masking the color. But the powdered form is often easier to find.

Other aromatic fixatives are the whole forms of vanilla bean, cloves, nutmeg, and cinnamon stick pieces. Penny Black in *The Book of Potpourri* (Simon and Schuster, 1989) also lists chamomile flowers, coriander seeds, angelica, sweet cicely, cumin, dried lemon verbena leaves, and sweet woodruff as easy-to-find fixatives. So when orrisroot is listed in a recipe, don't be afraid to substitute.

To make a dry potpourri, Black recommends mixing the essential oils and any spices or heavily aromatic materials with the fixative and rubbing with the fingers before adding the petals, flowers, and other delicate matter.

I usually forego adding a fixative unless it's a scent I particularly need for my blend, preferring to create new potpourris as the old ones lose their appeal.

I once planted Florentine iris in my garden specifically for use as a potpourri fixative, letting the clumps grow and mature until I deemed them large enough to dig up, chop, and dry the roots. But despite the fact that the flowers are neither colorful nor particularly exciting, I hadn't the heart to kill the plants and left them in the cutting garden to live out their natural life cycle in their own unobtrusive way.

Beyond the Garden

Lavender and Old Roses

WHAT YOU NEED

3 cups lavender buds

3 whole dried flowers, including 1 rose

1 cup rosebuds and rose petals

3 drops essential oil, all lavender, all
    rose, or a combination of both

Low, wide container

WHAT YOU DO

1 Mix the essential oil with the laven-
der buds and place in the container.
This one is a silver breadbasket.
(See next page.)

2 Place a whole dried rose in the
center and two other whole
flowers on either side. Place the
rosebuds and petals in a pattern
around the mixture.

   Dried flowers that are less than perfect find a home
in this structured potpourri. It not only emits the
aromas of lavender and roses but is as decorative as a
flower arrangement in a vase.

   When you have more dried lavender buds than rosebuds, the lavender forms the base. When you have more
rosebuds than lavender, the rosebuds form the base and
the lavender buds hide among the petals. The "stews"
both look and smell good but are substantially different.

3 To refresh and release the aroma as the weeks go by,
gently reach in and bruise the lavender buds with your
fingers, stirring gently so as not to disturb the rose
pattern.

TIP: LAVENDER BUDS

**You can purchase lavender buds by the bag or produce your own
from lavender in the garden. Cut short stems for drying after the
buds have reached their most intense color but before the petals
have formed. The petals will turn brown as they dry, not a very
pretty sight. Hang the stems in small bunches in a warm, dark, dry
spot (see pp. 121–122 for instructions on air-drying). When completely dry in two to three weeks, hold a bunch over a big pot and
gently rub your fingers along the stems, allowing the buds to
collect in the pot. When you have removed as many of the buds as
possible, remove any large pieces of leaf or stem that have also
fallen in.**

Fragrance and Taste

VARIATIONS ON A THEME
More petals and fewer buds, this lavender and old-rose potpourri changes the recipe only slightly, using whatever is available. The yellow rose petals pop out among the more subdued lavender. The red roses here are 'Mercedes,' the same ones used in the fresh Winter Rose Wreath on pp. 28–29.

Beyond the Garden

Where's the Scent?

Hydrangea needs a little help in the scent department.

WHAT YOU NEED

a bunch of your favorite aromaless flowers such as pink hydrangea

rose potpourri

any glass or plastic jar that holds water and is wide enough for a pin holder

large glass salad bowl or punch bowl

pin holder or "frog" to hold the stems

floral preservative

floral shears

WHAT YOU DO

1 Put the glass or plastic container inside the big bowl. Insert the pin holder in the bottom of the smaller container. Add water to which floral preservative has been added according to package instructions.

If you want first aid for aroma-challenged flowers, incorporate potpourri into your floral arrangement. The rose potpourri serves two purposes: it imparts a delightful aroma to a simple bunch of pink hydrangea and it hides the mechanics inside the water container. Since the potpourri is not the main visual feature, its aroma counts more than ever. Admirers will be enchanted by the overall presentation rather than the individual elements.

2 The rose potpourri is a simple mixture of dried rose heads, purple larkspur, and pink pepper berries with a few drops of rose essential oil. Use any favorite combination of scents and roses.

3 Add potpourri to the big glass bowl.

4 Strip the leaves from the bottom of the hydrangea and most of the other leaves as well, leaving only a few.

Fragrance and Taste

5 Stand the hydrangea stems in the water, holding them in place with the pin holder.

VARIATIONS ON A THEME

I got carried away in the garden of photographers Alan and Linda Detrick when we were photographing this arrangement. Planning to use only hydrangea for the simplest kind of "stuff-it-in-a-vase" arrangement of pink hydrangea with potpourri, the other midsummer lavenders and pinks seduced me. First some purple coneflowers, then some stems of butterfly bush. Finally a few stems of astilbe and roses. I somehow resisted the phlox that were in full bloom, the pink lilies, and the Russian sage just coming into color. The potpourri was getting more obscured with every new flower, the container was getting crowded, and worst of all, I was cheating. I wasn't even conditioning the flowers as I greedily ran to cut and add to the arrangement.

If you ever cheat in this way, make sure that you add water to the jar very frequently. This number of flowers will drink a small container dry in about an hour on the first day and will continue to drink thirstily until fully saturated. Even then, many flowers in a small container mean that you will be busy watering daily for the life of the arrangement.

Beyond the Garden

Bridal Potpourri

The mother of the bride is on the verge of heaving a huge sigh of relief. The wedding was filled with warmth, beauty, and joy. As the bride leaves for her honeymoon she tosses last-minute instructions. "One last thing, Mom, please dry my wedding bouquet."

Shock spreads over the mother's weary features. If the drying and preserving wasn't preplanned along with the rest of the wedding, the flowers will wither and die long before the mission is accomplished. Drying flowers to re-form into a bouquet means taking flowers at their peak and processing them promptly. The bouquet will look lively, not spent, only if dried immediately by skilled hands.

A wonderful option is bridal potpourri, demanding the least of both the flowers and the mother of the bride, and providing a keepsake to treasure for years. If the roses are edged in brown, the peonies have started to shatter, the orchids have lost major petals, and the trailing ferns have almost disappeared, all will still be well.

WHAT YOU NEED

bridal bouquet, centerpiece, or altar arrangement

rubber bands

floral shears

mixing bowl

2 cups dried aromatic herbs such as lemon verbena or scented geranium leaves *or* 4 drops essential oil or perfume

decorative bowl

WHAT YOU DO

1 Disassemble the bouquet. Discard any wire, tape, or foam. Save special ribbon for another use.

2 Divide flowers and leaves into small bunches (half a handful each), wrap in rubber bands, and hang to dry in a warm, dark, dry spot (see pp. 121–122 for drying instructions). For the most lifelike appearance, use a desiccant such as silica gel or kitty litter instead, following the directions on pp. 125–126.

3 In two to three weeks the flowers will be dry. Take them down and examine them again. Set aside the best looking whole flowers, for example whole roses with their stems intact.

4 Cut off the stems of the other flowers and leaves and discard.

5 In a bowl mix leaves, petals, buds, and partial pieces of flowers. Add the aromatic herbs or oil and mix well. Pour into the decorative bowl.

6 Steam open the whole roses on stems (see p. 129 for instructions).

7 Cut off stems. Place the reserved whole flowers on top of the potpourri.

8 Tell your daughter in advance of your clever idea so as not to shock her. Await praise for your ingenuity.

Winter Spice

Comforting aromas of spices and evergreens conjure up images of sitting by a cozy fire during the holiday season. The color scheme for this potpourri is abstracted from winter in the forest: the green of the conifers, white of the birch, brown of the tree trunks, and red of the berries. Come spring, replace it with a lighter scent: a potpourri of bright spring fragrances and colors.

This potpourri could be mixed up and placed in a big brandy snifter or laid out in a quasi-pattern with layers of botanicals as I did here. The color of the plate adds warmth to the design.

Beyond the Garden

WHAT YOU NEED

(Measurements are approximate and can be varied.)

½ C. whole cloves

1½ C. small conifer cones such as white spruce or hemlock

6 drops essential oils: 3 each of rose and patchouli or another favorite

glass mixing bowl

decorative plate or container

4 C. loosely packed fresh or dried juniper clippings with berries

8 cinnamon sticks

10 dried Queen Anne's lace flowers

1½ C. whole dried rose heads or petals

WHAT YOU DO

1   Put cloves and cones in a glass bowl and drop on the essential oils. Mix lightly and tightly cover with plastic wrap for a few hours to allow the oils to be absorbed.

2   Layer the juniper on the plate or in the container, then distribute the cinnamon sticks over it.

3   Cover with a layer of Queen Anne's lace. Then toss on the cones and cloves.

4   Finish with the roses on the top layer. I selected this particular variety of rose, 'Mercedes,' for the color. It has no natural aroma when dried. The purchased essential rose oil provides the scent.

TIP:

Mix oils with hard elements such as cloves, bark, cones, and cinnamon sticks, which will readily absorb it. More-fragile petals may be stained by the direct addition of oils. It's better to let them pick up the fragrance gradually after the layers are formed.

VARIATIONS ON A THEME

As with any potpourri, proportions aren't critical and substitutions may be readily made. If you're saving your precious roses for another project or have just run out, replace them with another dried red botanical. Here I've chosen a few heads of brilliant cockscomb as a stand-in. The large heads are easily broken into several pieces to distribute throughout the plate.

Fragrance and Taste

Using Fragrant Roses

Plant old roses such as *Rosa gallica* 'Officinalis,' the apothecary rose, for making rose water or other scented medicinals. The aroma and flavor increase with drying.

Plant *Rosa damascena*, damask roses; *R.* x *bourboniana*, bourbon roses; and *R. centifolia*, cabbage roses, for heavily scented petals, useful in attar of roses, potpourris, oil infusions, and other scented products.

To make rose water, place a pound of aromatic petals in an enamel or stainless-steel saucepan. Cover with water, preferably distilled. Bring to a boil then turn off heat and let stand for two hours. Strain in a fine sieve or cheesecloth. To make a stronger infusion, repeat the first step, using the already scented water. Some herbalists use very warm water and steep the petals in a glass jar in the sun all day, as if making sun tea. Use rose water as a final hair rinse or mild astringent for the face.

To make rose oil, take two cups of freshly picked aromatic rose petals. Place in a glass bowl and pour two cups warm olive oil, safflower oil, or unscented baby oil over them. Let steep for several hours then strain through a sieve or cheesecloth. Steeping the infusion in the sun makes the mixture stronger. Dab fragrant oils on the skin.

Both rose water and rose oil are prettier if made from red roses, which impart a pink blush to the finished product. Pink, yellow, or white roses sometimes give the water or oil a brownish tinge. Bruising the petals before infusing them releases more scent into the mixture.

In olden times women made scented rose beads using about a half bushel of fragrant rose petals picked fresh. These were ground in a mortar and pestle and the paste simmered in an iron pot with water. The reaction of the petals with the iron imparted a dull black color by which the beads were known. The paste was ground and simmered with water several more times, then beads were formed with the paste, which had a claylike consistency. To shape the beads, women dipped their fingers into oil and rolled the paste to the desired size, piercing the beads with a thin twig which was left in place. The beads shrank during the drying process and had to be turned regularly to enlarge the holes. When fully dry, beads could be polished and strung to wear as a necklace. The first rosary beads were probably made in this way.

Rose petals were also combined with other herbs and spices including cloves and cinnamon to make small linen sweet bags to hang around the neck and sachets to perfume cupboards and drawers. In the days when it was the custom to go months without bathing, such sweet bags and perfumes were more of a requirement for social interaction than the niceties they are today.

Beyond the Garden

Using Edible Roses

Use only organically grown roses for cooking. Roses grown for the floral trade are heavily sprayed with lots of things that are not meant to be ingested. This warning applies to other flowers, such as orchids and carnations, as well.

Cut off the bottom white portion of rose petals before continuing with any tea or jam recipe or sprinkling them on desserts. The white part is usually bitter and will mar the overall taste.

Strain tea or juices for jams made of rose hips to eliminate irritating fibers.

Plant *Rosa rugosa*, the Japanese rose, for its large hips high in vitamin C. Plant *Rosa canina*, the dog rose, for the same purpose. A tea made from its leaves is a mild laxative.

Sprinkle rose petals in wine coolers and fruit punch for decoration and flavor. Or freeze petals, semiopened buds, or small whole roses in ice cube trays with water and use in the same way. Sprinkle fresh aromatic petals on the serving table or tray as well.

Mix red rose petals with the white bottoms removed into herbal butters to improve their appearance and add an unusual flavor note.

Sprinkle organically grown rose petals on salads, including fruit salads. Other colorful and flavorful salad additions include nasturtium, borage, lavender buds, lemon marigold petals, and carnation petals. They are also a lovely garnish on any dessert plate.

ROSE JELLY

To balance the astringent qualities of rose petals, sugar is used in equal quantities in most recipes for jellies and jams. Here's a modern version of an old-time recipe.

3 C. fresh, aromatic red rose petals

1 ½ C. white grape juice

½ C. water

3 C. sugar

1 pkg. liquid fruit pectin

1   Trim off the white part of the petals, wash and drain. Bruise them with a fork, then combine with the juice in a stainless or enamel saucepan. Bring to a boil and simmer ten minutes. Discard the petals. Strain in a sieve or cheesecloth.

2   Return flavored juice to a clean saucepan with water and sugar. Add pectin according to package directions.

3   Pour into jam jars until set. Cool and refrigerate. If you're not going to bother with sterilization, freeze extra rose jelly or use within two weeks.

ROSE SUGAR

Rose sugar was made by pounding white sugar with double its weight of rose petals using a mortar and pestle. Today it is made by steeping dried petals in a closed jar of sugar for about a month until the aroma permeates the sugar. Strain in a coarse sieve if desired.

ROSE SYRUP

1   To make rose syrup, combine a pint of strong rose water and a pound of sugar; stir to dissolve.

2   Simmer while stirring and boil down to half its quantity. This flavorful syrup will keep for several days if refrigerated.

3   Pour over pound cakes, crepes, and other desserts.

Beyond the Garden

Special Occasions

To every grateful sound of earth and air;
Pausing at will our spirits braced, our thoughts
Pleasant as roses in the thickets blown,
And pure as dew bathing their crimson leaves.

— William Wordsworth

A grand event demands a grand arrangement, making flowers part of the celebration. Even if your garden has never looked better and your roses are at their peak, a creation in a large urn or footed jardiniere adds to the sense of occasion at a garden reception. Whether you're responsible for only one creation or for designing and making all of the table centerpieces, this is no time to stint.

Other times the event may be dinner at home with best friends, a joyous party *à deux*, or a family celebration. Whatever the gathering, quantities of flowers highlight the occasion.

Chapter 7

Rosa Grande

Purchase or pick flowers several days in advance so they are opened and well conditioned before tackling the project. For an arrangement of this size it's best to construct it in place. Select an elevated spot like a pedestal, niche, or garden wall. Or make your own pedestal from a rock, a wooden box, or another urn upended.

Indoors select a site where the arrangement will be spotted immediately. Outdoors, the flowers will last longer if shaded for most of the day. Once you have selected the site you'll know whether this is to be viewed from all sides or only three.

Choosing the Flowers

Ordering Ahead

For a wedding or grand party you may know the date six months or more in advance. I have frequently had time to select and plant seeds in my cutting garden so the flowers would bloom when I needed them. But if that isn't possible, your favorite florist will be happy to order what you want. Make sure to check with her several weeks in advance and place an order so they are delivered about three days before your party. Discuss what substitutes you'd like if certain flowers aren't available.

Color

The color of the arrangement is often predetermined, dictated by the wedding colors selected by the bride, school colors for a graduation, or a combination to complement your interior decor. Here I've kept to an

the Garden

analogous color range of blues, lavenders, and purples. Narrowing the color range makes the selection and construction easier.

Habit

Since the urn will be raised, I like some material to droop down over the sides of the container. Here the pink pepper berry and the sprigerei fern perform that function. Other trailing greens such as ivy, vinca, green or purple amaranth would be excellent substitutes. Check with your florist as to what will be available. Roses are available year-round but particular varieties may not be.

Mass

A grand arrangement needs some big flowers or big groupings of flowers. Single stems of lavender, for example, would look completely ridiculous or get lost. Here I've used peonies, giant allium, and hydrangea to provide the mass. The roses are fully opened to look larger than they do at bud stage, though they won't last so long after the party.

Number

I analyze, plan, and count, then deliberately order or cut 20 percent more than I think I'll need. I subscribe to the "just in case" philosophy of life; too many are better than too few. Flowers must be well conditioned for this arrangement, and even if you have lots of additional blooms handy in your own garden, it's poor practice to cut and immedi-ately stuff them in the arrangement if you run short. Drooping flowers may be the result.

Leftovers will not go to waste. Make a quick, casual arrangement for the powder room or other bare spot.

Grooming and Conditioning

See pp. 118–120 for instructions. All this work is done ahead of time, making the actual construction go faster. When you start the arrangement you will have to recheck the grooming, removing any petals that have turned brown or any excess foliage and shortening stems as necessary. Leave flowers in the buckets of water until you actually need them.

Filler

There is no filler foliage in this arrangement, but there well could be. To cut down on the cost of the arrangement, cut foliage from your garden. Some favorites are large hosta leaves, boxwood, lady's mantle, and artemisia. You probably have favorites of your own, depending on where you garden, perhaps large lotus leaves or palmetto fronds? Greens from the florist include the ever-popular lemon leaf, ginger foliage, and all manner of ferns.

WHAT YOU NEED

1 bunch pink pepper berries

1 bunch springerei fern

5 stems blue hydrangea

7 peonies

5 giant allium

20 stems larkspur

10 delphinium

4 dozen lavender roses, mixed 'Prelude' and 'Blue Curiosa' or just one kind

large urn and liner, if needed

plastic pot that fits inside urn

masking tape

2–3 blocks floral foam

floral scissors

WHAT YOU DO

1 The urn must be able to hold water. If it has a hole in the bottom, insert another pot as a liner. Invert a plastic pot inside as a platform for the foam.

2 Soak floral foam for at least an hour, then place in the container so it rises two to three inches above the rim. This simple step of cutting the foam higher than the rim will add immeasurably to the arrangement, allowing you to add

Special Occasions

stems at many different angles. Use masking tape or other sticky tape to secure the foam to the container. (See p. 85 for a picture.)

3   Much of the material is clustered for this arrangement. Insert the drooping stems first, here the pepper berries and the fern. They will be much harder to add at the end after all the other flowers are in place. As you make the arrangement, try to cut and place a stem only once. If you must remove a stem, recut the bottom before reinserting it in another position.

4   Next insert the biggest flowers: hydrangea, peonies, and allium. Again they are clustered rather than scattered throughout. As you work on the arrangement, keep circling around the urn so flowers are placed evenly and there are no visible bare spots.

5   Add the larkspur and delphinium, saving the roses for last.

6   Roses are added at the end so they will be sure to show and not get buried in the mass.

7   Water the arrangement each day until you take the flowers apart to discard.

TIP:

When making this kind of arrangement, the height should be approximately one and a half times the size of the container. Cut some of the stems of each kind of flower shorter and push them toward the interior of the arrangement. If you don't have everything blooming on the perimeter you will have a much more three-dimensional and natural look.

VARIATIONS ON A THEME

When it's not the season for blue hydrangea, add more larkspur, peonies, perhaps some lisianthus, and magenta roses such as 'Mascara.' Notice how the arrangement looks the same because of the color range yet different with a swap of some flowers.

TIP:

If you condition the roses you purchase while they're in bud and allow them to open in the bucket for two or three days before the party, the size of flowers will double. You can use about a third fewer flowers in the arrangement and enjoy the more powerful aroma and beauty from the unfurled blossoms.

Masses of Roses

Simple to construct but dramatic in appeal, this design of concentric rings of roses can be used as a centerpiece on party tables, to grace the place-card table, or at home to greet visitors to town for a wedding.

Select a round watertight container or a handle-less basket with a liner. The number of roses you need of course reflects the diameter of the container and the size of the flowers. The roses are in three tints of the same color and can be three yellows, three reds, three oranges, etc.

WHAT YOU NEED

16 light-pink roses such as 'Livia'

13 medium-pink roses such as 'Dolores'

14 dark-pink roses such as 'Mascara'

floral preservative

2–3 blocks floral foam

paring knife

round watertight container, this one is 7" in diameter

masking tape or floral sticky tape

floral shears

Beyond the Garden

WHAT YOU DO

1 Condition the roses (see pp. 118–120).

2 Soak the foam in water to which floral preservative has been added.

3 With the paring knife, cut the foam to fit to the edges of the container using a few large pieces. The foam should be two inches higher than the lip of the container.

4 Tape the foam in place so it's more secure.

5 Start with the outer ring of flowers. Cut the stems on an angle to two inches long and insert them on an angle, going all the way around the rim of the container without crowding, but hiding the foam. Care in placement of the roses will result in a glorious arrangement.

For the next tier of flowers the stems will be two and a half inches long, then three inches long for the final two tiers. A single rose of the first variety completes the arrangement. Its stem is a little longer yet.

6 When you've finished the arrangement, add some extra water to the container. The short stems and the regular addition of water help the roses to last longer.

VARIATIONS ON A THEME

Plain roses are breathtaking, but add one additional element and you may like the arrangement even more. Here I used some leftover larkspur purchased for the Rosa Grande arrangement on pp. 86–88 and interspersed it among the tiers of roses. The deep purple color pops amid the pinks.

The colors were selected by the bride, pinks from light to dark, nothing too pale and nothing too boring.

She wanted roses, roses, roses with "something else" to provide interest. The bouquet was to look like it was hand tied, something to carry on her arm. But she wanted it to last long enough so her mother could take it home and preserve the flowers.

To make the bouquet last, it should be constructed around one of the plastic-backed floral foam holders available from a craft store or florist. They come in various sizes and shapes, both round and rectangular. The foam part is often removable. The plastic cage can be reused with a new piece of foam for the dried bouquet.

A real hand-tied bouquet looks completely natural, as if you stepped out to the garden to gather an armful of flowers and tied them casually with a bow. But by the end of a long wedding and reception, the flowers often look the worse for wear. Flowers inserted into wet floral foam will hold up beautifully into the next day, when they are ready to be dried for posterity.

While most of these flowers will be purchased, using even one peony from the garden will personalize the bouquet. As always select flowers that are available in season, here in late spring.

WHAT YOU NEED

1 peony

8 stems viburnum

10 stems snapdragons

10 stems pale-pink roses such as 'Livia'

10 stems pale-yellow roses such as 'Timeless'

10 stems sweetheart roses

1 bunch spray roses such as 'Majolica'

10 stems lisianthus

floral preservatve

floral foam in a plastic cage,
    3 ½" wide x 4½" long x 3 ½" high

floral shears

3 yards ribbon

8" floral wire

Wedding Bouquet

WHAT YOU DO

1 Condition the flowers as described on pp. 118–120.

2 Soak the floral foam in water with floral preservative added according to package directions for at least an hour; remove and drain. Hold the cage horizontally and vertically over the bucket until no more water drips out.

3 The length of the stems ranges from nine inches to three inches. As you cut the stems from the flowers, reserve them for later use.

4 Place the cage on a table, handle toward you. First you will insert flowers in the two sides, then the top and the face. Very few flowers will be placed on the bottom, because that's where the stems will eventually go.

5 Start with the peony, viburnum, then the snapdragons.

6 Continue with the larger roses. Fill in with the sweetheart roses, the spray roses, and the lisianthus at the end. Thus far the bouquet could easily pass for a centerpiece, especially if the handle is hidden.

7 Select eight of the nicest stems from the discard pile, and cut them twelve to fourteen inches long. If you are including some of the rose stems, be sure to cut or break off the thorns.

8 Insert them at the bottom of the foam, near where the handle emerges. They should look like they are coming from a central point.

9 Make a bow with five to seven loops and secure it with the wire. Before tying on the bow, hold the bouquet in the upright position and let any excess water drain again. Wipe plastic cage dry with a rag. This is no time to be dripping water on a bridal gown.

10 Tie the bow around the handle and the stems. Fill in any bare spots with small stems of flowers.

TIP:

With wet floral foam and a large quantity of flowers, this is not a lightweight bouquet. It is also not meant to be thrown, but meant to be preserved. Construct a smaller hand-tied bouquet for throwing, if desired.

TIP:

Purchase the most beautiful ribbon you can find in a color that looks nice with the dress; deciding between cream and stark white is a main consideration. No matter how the ribbon is decorated, or even if utterly plain silk, selecting a ribbon that is wired at the edges will make the job of forming a professional-looking bow much easier. No matter what the project—wedding bouquet, wreath, or topiary—nothing cheapens a design faster than a cheaplooking ribbon. The ribbon should not be an afterthought, but an integral part of the plan and suit the purpose of the arrangement.

Special Occasions

Mantel Mélange

Red is the color of passion and love, of fire, emotion, and heat. For a winter holiday or special event, shades of red are all that's needed to jolt the viewer out of complacency. Red roses create a spark that ignites a fire even when the fireplace itself has gone cold.

Sweep your current display from the mantel. Gather an assortment of red glass together: stemware, tumblers, plates, vases, pitchers—whatever you can find in cupboards, at flea markets, and in shops. In the months leading up to Christmas, it's easy to find all sorts of containers. Each container holds but one variety of flowers, making arranging a snap. It's merely a matter of deciding how short to cut stems and moving containers around until you're satisfied.

The color tones here group around the true reds shading toward orange, rather than the pink- or blue-reds such as fuchsia. I scoured the flower markets for similar flower tones.

Beyond the Garden

WHAT YOU NEED

An assortment of red flowers; some possibilities in addition to large and small roses are Gerber daisies, tulips, amaryllis, hypericum (St. John's wort), calla lilies, gladiola, carnations, Peruvian lilies, and in-season zinnias, dahlias, anemone, ranunculus, and cockscomb.

floral preservative

red glass containers of different sizes and shapes

glass plate (optional)

floral shears

glass marbles or small pin holders

a few strands of raffia

florist water tubes with caps

candles: tapers, pillars, and votives as desired, in holders

foliage as desired

WHAT YOU DO

1   Condition the flowers as described on pp. 118–120, taking care to recut the stems of the roses in a basin of water to start the conditioning process.

2   Group the containers on the mantel. Here the largest is in the center and the rest are placed in descending size on either side. If you have a plate, stand it behind several of the shorter containers.

3   Fill the containers with clean water to which you've added floral preservative in the recommended amount (following package directions).

4   Assess the containers and plan the flowers for each, making a list if necessary. Any extra containers can hold votive candles.

5   Place the largest flowers first, here the Gerber daisies, amaryllis, and large bunch of twenty roses. Trim stems as necessary. Here the four stems of amaryllis are held in place with glass marbles and the stems are tied together just under the flowers with a handful of raffia. The amaryllis are now the tallest element on the mantel, and the size descends from there.

6   Now add the other flowers, one variety to each container. The parrot tulips have their own tumbler to show off their fancy frills. The plain tulips rest separately in their glass. I have only five of the dark rose 'Black Beauty,' so they must be cut short to fill their glass.

7 These calla lilies grew on long curving stems, so I inserted each in its own floral tube and placed it along the mantel where it could drape down and break the strong horizontal plane.

8 Place votives in any leftover glassware and place tapers and pillar candles well away from any delicate petals or foliage.

9 Add foliage to any container as desired. Here some asparagus fern, cut from an exuberant houseplant, joins the biggest bunch of roses.

VARIATIONS ON A THEME

If it's December and a holiday party is in the offing, group the flowers as above, but omit the calla lilies or place them in another red glass vase. Now lay some branches of evergreens among the containers and add a few sprigs to some of the vases. Scatter conifer cones and curls of birch bark among the greens and wind two and a half yards of half-inch ribbon around and between the elements. Remember to keep lit candles well away from flowers, greens, or ribbon.

This design also works well running down the center of a large buffet table on a fabulous strip of burgundy damask.

TIPS:

To vary the height of containers, upend a tumbler and stack another on top of it to make a taller vase.

The various species will begin to fade at different rates. On this mantel, the tulips may be the first to go. Keep your mantel design looking fresh by gently removing any vase with sad flowers and consolidating the others toward the center. Also groom individual blossoms that fade, like one amaryllis flower, by snipping it off with floral shears. By paying attention to individuals, you enhance the beauty of the whole and will probably be enjoying a few red flowers two weeks after you started your construction.

NOTE:

It's true my plan was to limit my palette to bright reds. But on the day I shopped for flowers for this design, I discovered calla lilies in deep, rich mahogany—almost black—and I couldn't resist their form and curvaceous stems. I thought they would provide an interesting contrast to the intensity of all the bright reds. I grabbed two purple glasses from my kitchen cupboard to balance out the dark color I was introducing.

Beyond the Garden

Don't Be a Square

When the mood strikes to make something special for yourself, celebrate with a large and impressive rose wreath in an unexpected shape.

I have a secret that will change your wreathmaking life. It's called galvanized wire and sells for about ten cents a yard. It's as close as your nearest hardware store, often in hundred-foot rolls. With it you can make wreath bases for dried flowers in almost any size and shape. When you want to make a rectangular wreath, getting the right size frame is easy. From miniature to giant, square, oval, heart, or even triangle and hexagon, you can do it.

Dried materials are so light that this easy-to-bend wire holds up well. For heavy materials, such as fresh evergreens, you may need to double or triple the strands.

WHAT YOU NEED

1 big bunch fresh salal leaves, also called lemon leaf. (The bunch used here is packed for wholesale. Any florist can order one for you.)

6 dozen air-dried roses in assorted colors and sizes

16-gauge galvanized wire

wire cutters

ruler

floral shears

reel of florist wire

2 yards fine satin ribbon

glue gun and glue sticks

nail or wreath hanger (optional)

Special Occasions

1 Measure the amount of wire you'll need for the frame and add three inches for wrapping the ends together. (See tip on p. 97 for measurement instructions.)

2 Cut off the desired amount of wire from the reel and bend it into shape, securing the ends. There are as many ways to secure the ends as there are ending off thread when you're sewing. My favorite method is to bend each end of the wire backward one and a half inches, forming a hook. Then hook the two ends together. Wrap the loose wire around the main frame to finish it off.

3 Cut the salal into pieces about eight inches long. Save any single leaves and the bare stems. Let them dry in a pile on your worktable for fill-ins later.

4 Divide the salal into two piles. This helps you to budget your materials and not run out of leaves. One pile is for the first half of the wreath; the other pile is for the second half. Some people will do better with four piles to help plan ahead by working one-quarter of the wreath at a time. You know who you are! Experienced wreathmakers will be able to eye the pile and work accordingly.

5 Tie the reel wire onto the frame. Bundle three or four stems of fresh salal leaves and wrap them tightly to the frame with the reel wire. As the salal dries it will shrink and loosen, so it must be tight at the start.

6 Take a second bundle of salal and place it on top of the stems in the first bundle, wrapping tightly in place. Go all the way around the wreath with the salal.

7 Cut off a small piece of reel wire and bend it onto the back of the frame to make a hanging loop if desired. This step is not necessary if you know you'll be hanging the finished wreath from a nail or wreath hanger.

8 Allow the wreath to dry, then tie the ribbon in a simple bow and attach it to the top of the wreath with a piece of reel wire. I prefer to do this before decorating so the ribbon will be an integral part of the design, not an afterthought.

9 If you feel the stems have gotten too loose in spots, gently turn the wreath over on the table and slip a few pieces of the extra dried salal under the wire. This will immediately correct the problem.

10 Glue extra leaves in any bare or skimpy spots.

11 Steam open air-dried roses following steps on p. 129. They will almost double in size. If you are working with freeze-dried roses, steaming will harm them.

12 Glue roses around the wreath with the glue gun, starting with the largest blooms and ending with small buds.

13 Trim the ends of the ribbon as necessary after you evaluate the completed design.

TIP:

Start with an eight-by-ten-inch wire frame (thirty-nine inches of wire: thirty-six inches plus three inches for the wrapping) to make a sixteen-by-twenty-inch finished wreath. Salal is so bulky that the finished wreath doubles in size. Make sure when you put the first bundle on the frame that you let the leaves extend beyond the frame and that you wrap only stems to the frame.

If you were using more-delicate materials, the wreath would grow substantially less, but at minimum you should allow for three inches of "growth" per side.

TIP:

I prefer to make the wreath base with fresh salal, which dries easily in place. Let the wreath lie flat on a worktable for one to two weeks where it will gradually get pale and curly. Once it's dry you can decorate the wreath with the bow and roses. Make the wreath extra full because the leaves will shrink slightly as they dry.

TIP:

Purchase roses for drying when they're on special sale, never right before a big holiday when prices rise. Air-dry as you get them and store them for up to six months in a dry place with low light until you've gathered enough for a big wreath. Here I've used about six dozen. If you have fewer roses, cluster them at the top near the bow and call it a salal wreath with rose decoration. I promise it will be delightful. Or scatter roses throughout the wreath and select other favorite dried flowers to join them.

Special Occasions

Beyond the Garden

Tips for Growing Roses

No more be grieved at that which thou hast done:
Roses have thorns, and silver fountains mud;
Clouds and eclipses stain both moon and sun,
And Loathsome canker lives in sweetest bud.

— William Shakespeare, Sonnet XXXV

Hundreds of gardening books cram the shelves of bookstores and libraries with detailed information about varieties of roses and how to grow them. This is not such a book. In this book I've focused on how to use the roses in your home after you pluck them from the garden or bring them home from the flower shop. But I couldn't resist passing on some tips from gardeners who are highly opinionated about the best way to grow roses. The tips are not meant to be all-inclusive. The local library is a wonderful resource for excellent garden books on roses. Also pay attention to instructions that come with your roses. Rose growers have a vested interest in making sure that you are successful, so they usually provide excellent instructions in both catalogs and with shipped orders.

Chapter 8

Beyond the Garden

Rose growers seem to be divided among those willing to keep up regular spraying programs to eliminate pests and diseases and those who aren't. I fall in the second category, but I admire the results of those who use integrated pest management systems. They use impeccable cleanup routines, handpicking of larger insects, introduction of beneficial insects such as ladybugs, and spraying with insecticidal soaps. If they feel that stronger measures are necessary, they take them only as a last resort.

A climbing 'Blaze,'
just like my first rose bush.

When I was ten my father piled my sister and me into his '38 Pontiac and drove us to a hardware store where we were each allowed to select a rosebush to present to our mother on Mother's Day. In early May selection could be made only from the color photos tied to the bare canes, certainly not from our experience with roses. They cost a huge sum of money, each one dollar. We were astounded with the generosity of our hardworking and frugal truck-mechanic father. My sister chose a glamorous yellow tea rose, which bloomed but a few years, grew gangly, and died, a victim of benign neglect. I opted for the 'Blaze' climber, which flourished under a similar program, growing to cover the trellis and whole side of the back porch. Mother would sit on the porch surrounded by crimson flowers and humming bees, shelling peas for her family of six, seven, or eight—however many happened to be in residence. She was often accompanied in her task by her dear friend and next-door neighbor, Belle Frank, who would be stringing beans for her family of six. When I was well on my way to becoming a grandmother myself, that 'Blaze' was still climbing on the back porch of 5046 Nevada Street, admired by a progression of other families in residence.

With that 'Blaze' came my first lesson in rose growing. Selecting plants for the site and the gardener's temperament strongly influences the success of the plant. Even my big sister who was older and much smarter than I didn't have the powers to overcome her initial choice; a hybrid tea rose was a mismatch for the careless way our family gardened.

Before you walk away from planting roses because they're too hard, consider the advice of an experienced rosarian in a famous public garden: he told me if you live outside the hardiness zone for your favorite rose or have problems you can't cope with, treat your roses as annuals. Plant in the spring as early as you can for your zone, enjoy the season, and discard in the fall. You'll spend no more money than on a flat of annuals, you'll get as much show and maybe more pleasure. Be kind to yourself. Promote annual roses.

But for perennial pleasure consider these tips.

Growing Roses

Selecting Roses

1 Selecting a rosebush is a type of balancing act. But hardiness is the first imperative. Look for roses hardy in your horticultural zone. Buy from a **grower** (not just a garden center) that is in your zone. Especially in the northern United States, Canada, and the South, a grower in your zone will provide the shrubs most likely to succeed. Check the Internet and mail-order sources on pp. 134–135 for help in finding one.

2 Roses are described by their bloom sequence. For some, it's "once blooming," a three-week period in late spring or early summer. Others will rebloom in fall; yet others treat us with continuous bloom from late spring until fall. Before you discard any notion of planting a once-blooming rose, remember forsythia, lilacs, azalea, magnolia, and mock orange. Remember viburnum, rhododendron, dogwood, spring bulbs, and iris. All are "once blooming" even though they aren't burdened with the epithet. We eagerly await their show in season each year, even if the season lasts but a week. Anticipate the once-blooming rose varieties in the same way. All your expectations will be met. Then along with the Boston Red Sox fans, the Philly Fans, and the Chicago Cubs fans, repeat the mantra "just wait until next year."

3 Look for varieties that are labeled disease- and pest-resistant. These may not include your favorite hybrid tea rose but probably do include rugosa roses and many of the "old garden" or "antique" roses. If you are willing to spray on a regular basis— every week or two— then disease and pest resistance may not be an issue. Balance your desire for a particular variety with your willingness to do extra chores.

4 Balance your selection for color quality, rebloom, and fragrance. Many of the newer hybrid tea roses have been bred for qualities such as bloom size or color, and aroma has been sacrificed. If you hope to use your roses in potpourris, natural fragrance is important, but it can be enhanced with additions of aromatic oils.

5 Roses come in pots or bare rooted; mail-order sources usually feature the latter. Garden centers offer bare rooted roses as well as those in pots. Potted roses might have broken dormancy and may even be in bloom. Rose experts generally prefer to buy bare-rooted plants, which often look like dead sticks because they're dormant. Don't avoid these. They will adapt more readily to your garden soil and conditions and will, if planted correctly, develop strong roots in your garden.

6 Consider rugosa roses, which are known as much for their showy hips (the fruit of the rosebush) as for their flower. The hips, high in vitamin C, attract birds and are sometimes used in herbal teas and jams. The flowers are often single, or if doubles are only moderately showy.

Air-drying flowers and herbs in my old barn.

Beyond the Garden

7   Live in an apartment or condo where the only growing space is a terrace or deck? Select a small shrub rose such as 'Red Fairy' or 'Flower Carpet' to plant in a large tub, for example a half whiskey barrel or larger container. The rose will drape down over the sides of the container in a most attractive way and come back year after year.

8   Don't expect one rose variety to provide everything you crave in a shrub. Consider having three to five varieties or more, each providing a different quality. Pore over several rose catalogs, which are very informative about types of roses, and read the fine print. If it doesn't say "fragrant" or "aromatic," it isn't. If you don't care, by all means order.

9   Select a gorgeous climber such as 'New Dawn' or 'Autumn Sunset,' which are pest- and disease-resistant as well as fast growers, covering a trellis or fence in two or three years.

10 Choose a rugosa such as 'Fru Dagmar Hastrup' for its luscious hips, long-lasting color, and appeal to bird life.

11 Find out if there is a rose society in your area. Attend a meeting, get on their mailing list, and ask questions from the experts. Gardeners are renowned for their generosity in helping each other. Join the American Rose Society and study their *Handbook for Selecting Roses*. Canadian residents will find the help they need at the Canadian Rose Society (see p. 134 for contact information in the United States and Canada).

12 If you and some friends have shrubs that you love, trade cuttings of old roses. Take a cutting from wood that is not too hard and not too soft. Dip in rooting hormone and place in potting soil rich with organic material. Trading is a great way to own a fine selection of roses at little expense. You should have the first blooms in two to three years.[2]

13 It was once a custom in many families to pass along a rose cutting, sometimes called "pass-along-plants," for a bride starting her first home. Author Eudora Welty writes in *Delta Wedding* of Aunt Primrose saying to her niece, "I started you a cutting of the 'Seven-Sister'[3] rose the minute I heard you were going to be married."

14 Don't be seduced by a name. As with paint colors, roses are often named to evoke emotional responses in the buyer. Remember 'President Kennedy,' 'Princess Diana,' 'Billy Graham,' 'James Galway,' and 'Barbara Bush'? A rose sold in different countries undergoes a name change as it crosses the border. Having warned you of this, I confess I've always had a 'Peace' or 'Chicago Peace' in my garden, and it's not because the flower flushes from crimson to gold and the leaves are a dark leathery green but because of the name. And if someone sent me a gift of the English rose 'Ellen,' I'd treasure it.

15 Look for roses that are self-cleaning, where the petals drop as the flowers die rather than turning brown on the bush and clinging on, unyielding in death. 'Seafoam' is one of the worst offenders and other small shrubs may also disappoint in this way.

16 For homes with antique interest or other historic buildings, consider planting only old roses, forms that were around before the hybrid teas were introduced in 1867. Catalogs usually list them as "antique roses" or "old garden roses."

17 Garden rose varieties are usually not the same as those grown in greenhouses for the cut flower trade, so don't be surprised if you can't track down your favorite florist rose to plant at home. For cut flowers from your garden, plant any of the hybrid teas or 'Charles Austin,' 'Graham Thomas,' 'Rosa Mundi', 'Reine Victoria,' or 'Buff Beauty.'

---

2   See *Secrets of Plant Propagation*, (Story Publications), 1985 for specific instructions.

3   Probably the popular nineteenth-century red rambler *Rosa Multiflora platyphylla*.

Growing Roses

Planting Roses

1 Plant in full sun with excellent drainage. This is no time to be arrogant. Mother Nature doesn't care that you would love to have a fragrant rose blooming in the shade by your front door. Shade and roses generally don't go together. Six hours of full sun spring through fall is a basic requirement, with four hours an absolute minimum. A few roses are listed as shade tolerant; these fall into the "four hour" class. And even these can't tolerate deep shade. My 'New Dawn' climber, which got only four hours of sun, had a gorgeous flush of bloom but once a year, while those planted in full sun usually give bounteous bloom throughout the summer.

2 For climbers, make sure that the trellis is very strong and well away from the wall. My Poor 'America' fried against the heated stone of my southern exposure as I attached my first trellis directly to the stone wall of my home.

3 Plant roses in a formal or informal setting. If formal, plant roses at different sight levels: carpet roses as a ground cover; miniatures in pots; hybrid teas, floribundas, and hedge roses for the midlevel; climbers on arbors and trellises; and tree roses for the upper level.

4 With very few exceptions, I much prefer roses intermixed in a border with other shrubs, annuals, and perennials than by themselves in a formal rose garden. If you do want to plant them off by themselves, tea roses look much better if underplanted with perennials such as *Veronica* 'Crater Lake Blue,' woolly thyme, lemon balm, or lamb's ears. But roses don't like other plants to touch them and don't like competition from strong roots of other trees and shrubs, so give them a little space of their own.

5 Beware of standing water. Plant where drainage is excellent. Containers must have drainage holes and a light soil such as a sandy loam.

6 Before planting, soak the roots of bare-rooted roses in warm, not hot, water for eight to twelve hours. Some prefer to soak the entire plant including the roots. Keep the plant in the bucket while digging and preparing the hole.

'Flower Carpet' rose tumbles along a border.

7 In my youth the saying was "Plant a fifty-cent rose in a five-dollar hole." By the time I had my own home and garden the saying became "Plant a five-dollar rose in a twenty-dollar hole." As you read this, it may be "Plant a twenty-dollar rose in a fifty-dollar hole." The mandate is the same no matter the inflation rate. A fine hole, with fine soil, water, and nutrients at planting time will reap rewards later. Don't skimp here.

8 How deep do you plant? It depends on where you live. In cold climates, plant the bud union where the graft is made, two to six inches below soil level. The bud union is the swollen area between the roots and the canes. It's the place from which new canes will grow each year, and where hybrid and other roses are grafted onto stronger rootstock. It must be protected from extreme heat or cold. In a warm climate, plant the bud union at soil level. Read the instructions that come with the rose, call your local extension agent, ask a neighbor who grows roses successfully, or e-mail the nursery where your rose was grown. In short, get advice from a rose expert who knows your area. The American Rose Society has consulting rosarians in each part of the country who welcome the questions of members.

Growing Roses

Continuing Care of Roses

Mulching

1 Mulch to maintain moisture in the soil and reduce competition from weeds.

2 If winter temperatures regularly drop to 10–20° F, you must consider heavy mulching or planting roses as annuals. Plant climbers on pillars rather than trellises, so they can be wrapped completely.

3 Some avid rose growers in the cold north "tip" their roses for winter protection. They dig them up when the weather turns cold but before the ground freezes and lay them in trenches deep enough to settle roots and canes. Then they cover the roses with soil and mulch until spring planting season, when they are reestablished in the garden. At the Minnesota Landscape Arboretum, forty-six staff and volunteers tip 600 rosebushes each fall to preserve them over the winter.

Watering

Water roots with soakers, drip hoses, or a handheld hose at soil level. Watering foliage greatly increases the possibility of spreading fungus or disease. Roots need regular deep watering but leaves don't.

Feeding

1 Roses are hungry critters. Once the shrub is planted and the leaves break dormancy, start to feed, first at half strength until the leaves burst forth. Then fertilize regularly with your favorite flower food or special rose food according to package directions. Stop fertilizing garden roses and container roses after August.

2 Harried gardeners who want to fertilize their hungry roses just once a season should look for special delayed-release rose food such as 10-18-10.

3 Kelp preparations are favorites of some organic rose growers.

Pruning

1 Eager gardeners wielding their rose pruners in spring should remember: prune when the forsythia blooms. Directions on how to prune differ depending on the type of rose, but you should always cut one quarter inch above an outward-facing bud at a forty-five degree angle.

2 To prune deadwood from very prickly, larger shrubs such as rugosas, use one of the long-handled pruners with a telescoping handle. My old Fiskars Pruning Stik is my all-time favorite gardening tool because it handles chores like this with ease, saving me from grief amidst the thorns.

3 Cut out weak canes at the point of origin, suckers emerging from below the bud union, and canes crossing over and through the shrub. The rose should be left with an open, vaselike aspect.

4 After pruning, paint cut ends of canes with clear nail polish, white glue, or pruning goop to bar easy entry for rose cane borers.

Beyond the Garden

5. As flowers bloom and die, regular deadheading often encourages profusion of rebloom.

6. You may have to choose between more flowers and producion of rose hips. Deadheading spent flowers encourages more bloom but cuts away the ovary which may develop into decorative hips. To encourage hip production, stop deadheading by mid-August.

Pests and Diseases

1. The first and best defense against rose disease is a good offense. Get the best head start at planting time by choosing healthy stock appropriate for your horticultural zone. Plant immediately; don't let bare-rooted roses languish while you attend to other matters. Plant in the best sun, soil, and water conditions possible. Feed as recommended. Allow air circulation between plants. *Then* address problems as they occur. A plant unstressed by drought, shade, or lack of nutrients is far less prone to disease.

2. Rugosa roses with their wrinkled leaves generally are free from leaf blights that affect flat-leaf roses, such as black spot and mildew, and are not the first choice of chewing insects either.

3. Good hygiene matters more to roses than to many other plants. Pick up and burn or safely dispose of yellow or spotted leaves. Clean up in the fall even if you ignore the rest of your garden until spring. Don't add rose leaves to your compost pile. I sometimes grind them up in my garbage disposal if there are only a few or include them in the garbage pickup.

4. Keep off the roots. Standing on the soil around roses compacts it, preventing necessary air from reaching the roots.

5. Make the diagnosis before attempting the cure. Once you've determined that leaf blight is the problem, try this famous Cornell University organic fungicide, spraying it once a week: one gallon water, one tablespoon baking soda, one teaspoon canola oil or Ivory Liquid soap. This fungicide is particularly useful if you garden in a humid area. The oil or liquid soap helps spread the baking soda solution and makes it stick evenly to the leaves. There are many variation of this formula; some only use one-half teaspoon soap or oil. See what works best for you.

Some experts insist that fungicide must be sprayed regularly as a preventative measure before you see a problem. Make sure the plants are well watered before spraying.

6. Look for other organic products for black spot such as Rose Defense or other neem oil concoctions.

7. Japanese beetles a problem? I actually find it relaxing to visit my rosebushes in the early morning with a saucepan of hot water mixed with a little detergent. Hold the pot directly under a flower, then carefully bend the flower stem and tap. Beetles drop as soon as they're disturbed, and the pot will be there lying in wait. In Pennsylvania, July 4th was the signal for beetles to emerge and start munching.

8. Some gardeners swear that planting garlic as a companion plant to roses eliminates many insect pests and diseases such as Japanese beetles and black spot. And you'll get the fantastic taste of fresh garlic as a kitchen bonus.

9. If you don't want to spray at all, do as I do. Select the most disease-resistant plants you can, then learn to live with leaf drop.

Growing Roses

Types of Roses

Categorization of roses is somewhat confusing but simple definitions will help when you make your selections.[4] The American Rose Society maintains the official classifications. Their handy booklet, *Handbook for Selecting Roses*, rates 300 varieties for excellence and also describes the classifications (see p. 134 for contact information). Be aware that catalogs, garden centers, and growers sometimes use other classification characteristics.

Species Roses

These are wild roses that reproduce themselves from seed. They grow in many parts of the United States and Canada and in other parts of the Northern Hemisphere. They are either shrubs or climbers, with four- to eleven-petaled flowers. Species roses are used for breeding modern roses. They include *Rosa multiflora* and *R. rubrifolia*. There are about 200 species roses and thousands of natural or man-made hybrids. Species roses are listed by their Latin names.

---

[4] These listings are based on the American Rose Society classifications.

Some Popular Old Garden Roses

Old garden roses are naturally occurring crosses, mutations in the wild, or hybrids introduced before 1867.

Alba (*Rosa* x *alba*) – Usually white or pale-pink flowers, upright shrubs with heavy perfume. Excellent disease resistance and hardiness. Thought to be related to *R. canina*, the dog rose. Usually alba have gray-green foliage and few thorns, for example *R.* x *alba* 'Semi-Plena,' with lovely hips, used to produce attar of roses. Once blooming. Zones 3–9.

Bourbon (*Rosa* x *borboniana*) – Repeat flowering with delicious aroma. Flowers lush and many-petaled, often arranged in four sections and sometimes appearing in clusters. Glossy leaves. Popular in Victorian England and in France. 'Souvenir de la Malmaison' is a good example; it originated on the Ile de Bourbon in the Indian Ocean. Zones 5–6 to 10.

Centifolia or Cabbage Rose (*Rosa centifolia*) – Once-blooming, large, many-petaled flowers with heady aroma. One of the oldest species known. Matte, dark-green leaves. 'Village Maid' is an example. Zones 4–9.

China (*Rosa chinesis*) – First came to Europe from China where they had been grown for centuries. Repeat-blooming small shrubs, fragrance like crushed tea leaves, tender roses. Small glossy leaves. Example: 'Mutabilis.' Zones 7–10.

'Mutabilis' displays blooms with varying colors on the same plant, a China rose.

Damask (*Rosa damascena*) – Ancient shrubs with pink or white ruffled blooms, strong fragrance. Often repeat flowering in clusters of five to seven. Downy leaves. Example: 'Mme. Hardy.' Zones 4 or 5–9.

Hybrid Gallica (*Rosa gallica*) – Small shrubs with profuse bloom and excellent fragrance. Oldest of all garden roses. Example: *R.g.* 'Officinalis' is known as the apothecary rose: it had been used for medicinal purposes in medieval times. Once blooming. Rosette-shaped flowers. Zones 4–8.

Moss – Furry, mossy growth on buds, stems, and leaves. Double, fragrant flowers in clusters of three. Thorny and once flowering. Example: 'Mme. Louis Leveque.' Zones 5–9.

Noisette (*Rosa* x *Noisettiana*) – Repeat blooming, but susceptible to freezing. First bred in Charleston, South Carolina, a cross between the musk rose and a China rose. Usually considered a climber. Canes need support on trellis or arbor. Example: 'Lamarque.' Zones 7–10.

Other less-common species of old roses include Boursault, Eglanteria (sweet briar rose), Hybrid Perpetual, Hybrid Sempervivens, Hybrid Spinosissima, and Portland—named not after the city in Oregon but after the Duchess of Portland.

Some Popular Modern Roses

These roses were bred and introduced after 1867 when the first hybrid tea rose was offered. The date is an arbitrary designation made by rosarians, with some modern roses looking very much like old ones.

Floribunda and Climbing Floribunda – Clusters of small flowers all over the short, bushy shrubs. Useful for hedges and mass plantings as they are very disease resistant. One parent is the polyantha. Example: 'Angel Face.'

Grandiflora and Climbing Grandiflora (*Rosa gallica* 'Grandiflora') – Very large flowers singly or in clusters, usually with excellent rebloom qualities. Example: 'Queen Elizabeth.'

Hybrid Musk – Repeat, prolific bloom, somewhat shade tolerant and highly aromatic. Most bred in the first half of twentieth century. Example: 'Buff Beauty.'

Hybrid Tea – First introduced in 1867, now over 10,000 varieties named. Usually one flower to a stem on upright shrubs. High-centered, large flower, often used for display. Some have little or no fragrance despite the magnificence of the bloom. The most common florist rose. Excellent for cutting, producing more flowers all summer. Close-up of the flower gives better view than appearance of the entire shrub. Example: 'Secret.'

Miniature and Climbing Miniature – Natural dwarfs that grow on their own rootstock. The average height is eighteen to twenty-four inches, though there are climbers that grow to eight to ten feet as well as microminis averaging five to eight inches. Size of the flower is proportionate to the plant, somewhere between a dime and a quarter. Miniatures are often very hardy. They have their own aficionados, collectors, exhibitors, and award categories at rose shows. Example: 'Stardance.'

'Queen Elizabeth'

'Secret' Hybrid Tea: note the high center of the flower.

Beyond the Garden

Polyanthas – Were developed from a cross between climbing *R. multiflora* and a China rose. Sprays of small, single flowers that are repeat bloomers (remontant). Hardy and disease resistant, good for ground covers and the front of the flower border. Example: 'Mlle. Cécile Brunner,' the sweetheart rose. There is also a climbing variety of 'Mlle. Cécile Brunner.' They are sometimes planted together for continuous effect.

Rugosa Roses and Hybrid Rugosa (*Rosa rugosa*) – Rugosas are usually winter hardy through Zone 3. They are disease-resistant and drought-tolerant rugged shrubs. Many are very thorny. Known by their crinkled or pleated leaves and usually smallish flowers. Treasured also for their large and decorative hips. Native to the coasts of Japan and Korea. Example: 'F. J. Grootendorst.'

Shrub Rose – A catch-all category for varieties that don't fit easily into any other category. They vary in height, bloom, and most other characteristics but are usually hardy, disease resistant, and good landscaping plants. Example: 'Scarlet Meidiland.'

'Scarlet Meidiland,' a good performer.

Tree Roses (Standards) – These roses are produced by two grafts: the roots to the stem and the stem to the small bush on top. Very tender, often planted in pots for ease of winter protection or "tipped," in other words dug up and laid in trenches, well covered by soil and mulch until spring.

English Roses – Modern roses bred to combine the best features of old garden roses including disease resistance and scent. They were crossed with floribundas and modern hybrid teas by David Austin. Many have a shrubby habit. Example: 'Mary Rose.'

Roses are also categorized by:

SHAPE OF THE BLOOM: Shapes include bell, cup, urn, many-petaled, rosette, flat, quartered, and pompon.

TYPE OF FLOWER: Roses can be single with a single layer of petals, semidouble (ten to nineteen petals), double (twenty to twenty-nine petals), full (thirty to thirty-nine petals), or very full with forty or more petals.

TYPE OF COLOR: Colors can be single (solid), bicolor (front and back of petals are two distinct colors), multicolored (the color is transformed as the flowers turns from bud to full bloom), blend (two or more colors on one side of the petal), or variegated (striped).

SUBSTANCE: A characteristic of petals describing how much moisture they can retain. This in turn depends on the amount of starch in the petals. In very warm climates, flowers with excellent substance won't droop in the heat.

Favorite Roses and What Makes Them Special

Which of your children do you love best? What's your favorite book? Your favorite piece of music? How can one choose? When I started asking gardeners for their favorite rose, few wanted to name just one. Here are some favorites.

This list is highly idiosyncratic and in no way a scientific survey. It represents my own preferences and those of a group of garden writers whom I happened to be traveling with to visit some sensational public and private gardens. Ask fifty rosarians for comments on roses and you're likely to get eighty-four responses. As with all other plants, trial and error will make you an informed judge in your own garden.

When ordering, note the date of introduction. Since 'Peace' was introduced to a waiting world in 1945 and is still being sold amidst thousands of competitors, there must be a reason for its wild popularity.

Sixteen years ago I bought three 'Ferdy' to border my patio but when I went to reorder I couldn't find this variety. The rosarian at Wayside Gardens noted that more cuttings of that rose should be made because he liked it too, but it's still very hard to find despite being a brilliant bloomer and completely impervious to all pests and diseases. I'm ashamed to say that I rarely fertilized those shrubs, pruned only when I needed some canes for a floral design, and cut out deadwood about twice during my stewardship.

'Altissimo' – Single, flat, five-petaled flower with prominent golden stamens. Great disease-resistant, fast-growing climber, repeat blooming in a knockout crimson red. Zones 4–9.

'America' – Hardy climber with repeat bloom, a favorite since 1976 for its coral, multipetaled blooms. Dries a beautiful red. Zones 4–9.

'Autumn Sunset' – Climber with brilliant, ruffled golden blooms, flame-colored buds. Continuous bloom, winter hardy, and disease resistant. Can be grown as a large shrub rose as well. Zones 4–9.

'Betty Prior' – Popular hedge rose, a floribunda with single petals, good for northern climes but not the coldest. Award winner in 1993. Carmine buds, bright-pink flowers. Zones 5–9.

'Carefree Delight' – At three to four feet, a bushy shrub rose for the front of the border, carmine pink, flat flowers, excellent disease resistance. Zones 4–9.

'Constance Spry' – A David Austin English climber, soft-pink luminous flowers with a heavy myrrh fragrance. Grows also as a large shrub. Has but one period of bloom. Zones 4–9.

'Darlow's Enigma' – Pure white, semidouble flowers, winter hardy, disease resistant, heady and strong perfume. Tolerates some shade. Zones 4–10.

'Double Delight' – Hybrid tea that's undemanding for its class, All-America Rose Selection (AARS) winner in 1977, also winner of fragrance award from American Rose Society. Strong, spicy fragrance; cream flowers blush to crimson, each a different color combination. A personal favorite. Zones 5–10.

'Eye Paint' – From New Zealand, a single, flat, scarlet flower with a prominent white eye. Continuous bloom on a four- to five-foot shrub. A perfect cottage garden rose with its shiny, dark foliage. Zones 5–9.

'Ferdy' (also known as 'Ferdi') – Floribunda; a favorite shrub rose for ease of care and massed bright-pink blooms. Unusually abundant. Some books promise orange hips, but in sixteen years my three Ferdys never produced any. Zones 5–9.

Beyond the Garden

'Flower Carpet' – Ground cover rose to thirty inches high with profuse, ruffled, bright-pink flowers. Excellent for planting in containers such as a half whiskey barrel. It'll drape down and hide much of the sides. Repeat bloom all summer. It is known for its hardiness and disease resistance, but don't expect any fragrance. Zones 5–9.

'Fru Dagmar Hastrup' (also known as Frau Dagmar Hartopp) – Rugosa rose renowned for its hips since 1914; easy to grow; redolent with spicy fragrance; with five cupped pink petals, but thorny. Very cold tolerant. Zones 2–9.

'Graham Thomas' – English shrub rose with cupped, sometimes quartered flowers of golden yellow. Grows as a large bush or climber in warmer zones. Disease resistant and beautiful in an informal bouquet. Tea rose fragrance. Zones 5–9.

'Iceberg' – For an all-white garden; each stem bears a spray of ten to twelve blooms that develop over time. One stem makes a complete arrangement in a small vase. The more you cut the more develop. A three- to four-foot floribunda. Zones 5–9.

'Iceberg' graces the foreground of this photo.

Growing Roses

'Knockout' – A cherry-red shrub rose with continuous bloom. Some say it's the best new rose in fifty years and the most disease resistant. AARS award for 2000 and special ARS members' choice award in 2004 in Zones 5–9.

'Mr. Lincoln' – A hybrid tea wildly popular since 1964; rich, red, velvety petals with a strong perfume. Drying turns the petals black. AARS winner in 1965. Zones 5–10.

'Mutabilis' (also known as *Rosa* x *odorata* 'Mutabilis') – Train as a climber or tall shrub. Known for spectacular color changes blooming simultaneously. Changes from flame to copper, honey, yellow-orange, and red. An old China rose with early and continuous bloom. Zones 6–9.

'New Dawn' – A climber with good repeat bloom, blush pink flowers, cold hardy, disease resistant, tolerates a little shade but may then bloom only once. Beloved since 1930. Royal Horticultural Society award of merit. Zones 4–10.

'Peace' – The most popular all-time rose. A hybrid tea bearing large yellow flowers flushing to pink. Each a different combination of colors, changing in different light and temperature and as they open. Beautiful glossy dark-green foliage. Many international awards. Scions include 'Pink Peace,' beautiful for cut flowers; 'Chicago Peace'; and 'Climbing Peace.'

'Pink Meidiland' – Stunning, flat, single flowers; robust pink with white eye and coral rose hips starting in midsummer along with continuous bloom. Showy yellow stamens. Disease-resistant shrub rose. Zones 4–9.

'Queen Elizabeth' – Won the AARS award in 1955 and is still going strong. A grandiflora rose with clusters of bright-pink blooms on long stems. Great for cutting. Disease resistant. Strong upright stems make it a favorite tree or standard rose. Zones 4–9.

'Queen Elizabeth' above

'Pink Peace'

'**Red Fairy**' – Cultivar of the old favorite small shrub rose 'The Fairy'; a hardy polyantha with repeat bloom, used in the front of the border or as a ground cover. 'Red Fairy' has a more robust color than its somewhat bland parent and is more pleasing to my eye. Zones 4–9.

'**Suma**' – Small, low-growing rose, useful for ground covers and hanging baskets, also used as a standard or tree rose. Small, glossy leaves turn burnished red in fall. Profuse and continuous bloom of dark, dark pink to ruby with repeat bloom. Zones 5–9.

'**Therese Bugnet**' – Large, ruffled, double-pink blooms. Repeat-blooming upright shrub. Highly fragrant, with blue-green foliage. One of the hardiest. Zone 2–8.

'**Tropicana**' – Brilliant orange hybrid tea. Strong fragrance with repeat bloom. Dries to a clear bright red, my favorite garden rose for drying. Zone 5–9

'**Zephirine Drouhin**' – Antique climber (1868), heavy perfume, tolerates a little shade, almost thornless. Zone 6–9.

'Red Fairy' displays masses of small blooms.

Growing Roses

Beyond the Garden

Roses Preserved

The rose is fairest when 'tis budding new,
And hope is brightest when it dawns from fears,
The rose is sweetest wash'd with morning dew,
And love is loveliest when embalm'd in tears.

—Sir Walter Scott, Lady of the Lake

Chapter 9

Caring for Fresh Roses

Harvesting

Cut in the early morning, when moisture and sugar levels are high in the stem. Select flowers whose outer petals are just starting to unfurl. If buds are too tight when picked they may never open.

If you want several spectacular blooms for a special display or competition, it will be necessary to disbud, pinching out side buds to allow the center bud to develop into one larger flower. Disbudding should be done when buds are still forming. All the shrub's energy will then be forced into producing fewer but larger flowers. Use a sharp, clean floral knife or pruner to make the cut, protecting the shrub from infection.

Harvesting flowers from the garden is always a balancing act: you must cut the length of stem you want for an arrangement while leaving what is necessary on the plant for future growth and bloom. When you make the cut, try to leave two sets of five leaflets on the stem where new flower buds can develop.

Buying

Roses, like fresh produce, have a limited shelf life. If you buy roses from the florist the day they came in from the wholesaler and if the florist bought them from the wholesaler the day they came in from the grower, you have gained three to four days extra to enjoy them at home. It's perfectly all right to call your florist in advance and ask when the next delivery of roses comes in. Buy on the day of, not several days after the shipment. If you're in the shop and rose fever hits, pull a bunch out of the pail and examine the bottom of the stems. If they're discolored or, heaven forbid, slimy they've definitely been around too long.

However, I do see flower sellers on the streets of New York recutting old stems and discarding slimy ends, so this is not a foolproof method. Check the petals and leaves for signs of mildew, damage, or browning around the edges. The same guys cutting off the bottoms of old stems also keep removing old petals and leaves to give older flowers a face-lift. You wouldn't buy peaches with soft brown spots or green beans that are turning brown; exercise the same selectivity with flowers, and you won't be disappointed.

Conditioning

Conditioning is a general term that refers to pretreating fresh flowers in ways that will lengthen vase life. It starts at the commercial farms and nurseries where roses are grown. Growers from across the country as well as other continents try to get them to your city, wholesaler, retailer, and you in the best possible shape. Roses are shipped in cardboard cartons from Venezuela, Central America, Israel, South Africa, as well as the United States before arriving at the nearest wholesaler then retailer, where stems of fresh roses are recut and rehydrated in buckets of water to which floral preservatives and bactericides have been added. Retail florists are advised to test their tap water monthly with litmus paper for pH before conditioning roses, adjusting water acidity to between 3.5 and 4 using powdered citric acid. Acidity level of the water affects the ability of the roses to rehydrate.

This all happens before you even get the roses home. When you pick roses from your own garden, they go right into the conditioning bucket without being in cardboard boxes for days, so you get the freshest flowers imaginable.

When you get the flowers home from the florist or from the garden, always begin with conditioning.

1 Trim off all lower foliage that would stand underwater.

2 Fill an impeccably clean bucket or tall container with warm water to which you add a floral preservative according to package directions. To be effective you must use recommended proportions, not more or less. If you're buying from a florist, make sure they give you a pack or two of preservative with your bouquet.

Beyond the Garden

If you grow your own roses, these packs are readily available for purchase from florists. The floral preservative usually contains an antibacterial agent and the amount of sugar needed for full petal development.

3   Fill a sink with warm water. Recut each stem on a slant underwater with a sharp, clean floral knife or floral shears, removing one-half to one inch of stem. Immediately place the flower in the bucket of water. Cutting underwater prevents air from getting in the stem and blocking the uptake of water.

4   Allow the flowers to rest for four to six hours in a cool, dim spot before using them in any arrangement. The purpose of this procedure is to allow the roses to drink as much water as possible, especially important if you will making an arrangement in floral foam where water uptake is somewhat restricted.

Vase Life

Anyone who has ever observed a vase of roses is aware of "bent-neck syndrome." Among a dozen perky flowers, a few flower heads droop, as if hanging their heads in shame. This happens even though the flowers aren't very old. "Bent-neck syndrome" has two possible causes. The flowers were cut too early in their development, in a very tight bud stage when the top of the stem was still comparatively thin and weak, or air bubbles or foreign matter have gotten into the stem, blocking the uptake of water.

It's usually possible to recondition these flowers with drooping heads so they perk up again. Remove them from the arrangement. Fill a sink with water and recut an inch of stem underwater. As you cut you often see little air bubbles escaping in the water. Plunge the flowers immediately into a tall glass of very warm water and leave them there for four to six hours.

Most roses will rehydrate and look as good as new, then you can put them back into the arrangement where they'll happily join their comrades.

You may have noticed that some florists take measures to prevent "bent-neck syndrome" by wiring the flower heads of roses and other flowers such as Gerber daisies, which suffer from the same fate. Wiring rose heads forces them to stay upright mechanically, but few home flower arrangers want to go to this trouble, and the petals still suffer.

Harvesting for Drying

OTHER TIPS FOR PROLONGING VASE LIFE

1 When floral foam is used, insert the stems deeply into the foam and add more water daily.

2 Groom flowers before conditioning them by removing any torn or damaged petals or leaves. Damaged flowers are most susceptible to bacterial growth, and bacteria may spread by contact from one flower to another.

3 Always work with clean buckets, vases, and shears. Wash them with a little chlorine bleach solution from time to time.

4 Don't save and reuse green floral foam even though it may look useful. It's probably harboring germs from its last use. Always start with a fresh piece of foam for fresh flowers. To satisfy your frugality, you may reuse brown foam for dried flowers if the structure is still substantially intact.

5 Vase life depends upon freshness of the flowers and upon conditioning, but it also varies among flower varieties. One commercial rose grower suggests that you shouldn't compare natural differences in longevity among varieties but should be pleased when roses open from bud to full bloom to shattering, no matter how long that takes.

6 Keep topping off the water in the vase until you discard the flowers and replace it completely after three days (don't forget the floral preservative).

The goal of drying flowers is to preserve their color, form, and aroma. To this end, how and when you harvest most flowers from the garden can be as significant as how you dry them. Some flowers such as roses are very forgiving; if you miss harvesting the buds you can still harvest the flowers as soon as they open fully or at any stage along the way. Other flowers such as hydrangea and yarrow must be harvested for drying when they are fully mature, lest the structure shrivel as they dry. Flowers such as goldenrod, lavender, lamb's ears, and globe thistle should be cut at the bud stage so the petals don't brown or fluff out as they dry. Peonies should be dried when they are half open, between the tight bud stage where the air can't reach the center petals and the petal-dropping stage.

Roses are like peonies, in that fully blown roses will drop their petals. Harvesting for drying must take place before the flowers are full-blown, or you will have nothing but potpourri materials after the drying is complete.

Cut roses for drying when all traces of dew, rain, or other moisture is gone. Unlike harvesting for fresh flower arrangements, cutting roses for drying is not an early morning activity. Ideally you shouldn't harvest immediately after several days of hard rain. The plants will have absorbed extra moisture and may not dry as quickly. Sometimes, though, you may need to harvest even when the conditions are less than ideal. If I have roses that need to be picked on a certain day regardless of moisture, I cut them and shake off the excess water droplets, then bring the roses indoors and stand them in shallow buckets of water. Within a few hours, when all the rain has evaporated, I bunch the stems for hanging, drying stems as best I can with paper towels.

Freshness counts with roses from the garden or purchased from a florist. The "garbage in-garbage out" principle applies equally well to computers and drying flowers. If you try to dry roses that are faded or brown around the edges, you'll end up with faded, brown dried flowers. Don't even think of enjoying your Valentine's roses for ten days and then drying them as an alternative to the compost pile. Decide at the beginning if you want to enjoy them in the dried state, then divide the bouquet, keeping half fresh in a smaller vase and putting half to dry as soon as they begin to open up.

Beyond the Garden

Roses Preserved

Air-drying

As harsh as it sounds, once a flower is cut it is on its way toward decomposing. The principle behind drying is to stop the process of decay as quickly as possible. So drying should start soon after harvesting and be accomplished as quickly as possible.

With all of the moisture removed, in a dry atmosphere flowers can last indefinitely. Archeologists have discovered dried flowers and other plant materials while excavating tombs in Egypt, thousands of years after the blooms were buried with the pharaohs.

By far the simplest technique for preserving roses is to air-dry them; that is, hang them upside down in a warm, dark, dry spot. Start with small bunches of five or six stems. Remove the bottom foliage and wrap the bunch in a rubber band. It's best if the flower heads are not exactly at the same level so they aren't too crowded together. Then hang from a hook or paper clip that is unbent into an **S** shape. If you have several bunches of flowers drying at once, leave some space between the flowers for good air circulation. There is no need to strip off all the leaves; in fact, I always leave one or two sets on every stem. They usually come in handy in the design phase.

Roses will be completely dry in two to three weeks depending on the atmosphere and size of the rose. Miniature roses dry in about a week. Outer petals and leaves will dry first. The thick part of the rose near the base and the stems will dry last. Roses that are fully opened will dry faster than tightly furled roses where the air can't circulate around each petal.

And of course, smaller roses will dry faster than huge roses.

When flowers are totally dried they can be removed from their hangers and stored in a cardboard box until you are ready to use them in a design. If you box them before all the moisture is removed, they will mildew in their tight quarters—more fodder for the garbage or compost heap.

Warmth

The warmer the atmosphere, the faster the flowers will dry. Find an attic, a basement, a furnace room, even a closet: the warmest place in your house. Temperatures of 90° to 100° F are excellent but rarely found in modern homes. My old farmhouse had three main places for drying flowers: the unair-conditioned attic, the basement over the ancient furnace (which spewed out heat even during the summer), and the rafters of the barn. Most of the ordinary flowers were dried in the barn, where wires had been strung for the purpose and summer temperatures often reached 90° F or more. Roses, blue hydrangeas, and some other favorites were often treated to the less-humid atmosphere of the attic or furnace rooms. During cold of winter, purchased flowers must be dried in a heated area. Remember that heat rises so that even in a closet or garage, hooks, nails, or wire near the ceiling will be better than lower down.

Dried roses in a container; compare to fresh ones on page 119.

Darkness

Sun bleaches out and fades flower color. Flowers dried in the dark will have truer colors than those dried in the light. Sunlight is the worst possible condition both for drying and later for hanging or placing the dried arrangement. When you are searching for warm conditions, also take darkness into consideration. If not completely dark, look for a dim, mostly dark room. A sun porch is a poor choice because though warm, the ambient light is strong and will fade flowers fast.

Dryness

In New Mexico, Arizona, Southern California, or any of the desert areas, the humidity is so low that flowers seem to dry overnight. Bright strings of hot peppers hang on doors of many homes in the fall. These *ristras* dry quickly and are preserved for culinary use or decoration for years to come. When I tried stringing hot peppers from my garden in Pennsylvania and hung them by the kitchen door, the mold grew before the water evaporated, yet another experiment gone astray. Flowers need low humidity in the atmosphere as much as heat to help them transfer their moisture to the air. That's why commercial drying operations use dehumidifiers and fans in the drying process.

Select a place where the humidity is relatively low. A bathroom is a poor choice.

Pressing

Experience with pressing flowers often begins in childhood: daisies in the dictionary, buttercups among the yellow pages. Teachers assign fourth graders to scavenge for tree leaves, press and label them for the bulletin board or scrapbook. Students learn to differentiate oak, maple, elm, and ginkgo or their local natives. This time-honored method of preserving flowers and leaves still works if you don't mind your books becoming discolored, but a few improvements help the process immensely.

Pressing Flowers

Making the Press

You can purchase a flower press in a craft store or make your own from scrap lumber. My favorite press is made from two pieces of half-inch-thick unpainted plywood, twelve-by-twenty inches. I drilled a hole in each corner, one-half inch from the edge, and bought four two-inch-long bolts and wing nuts to tighten the press. It's rough, not fancy, but the size is perfectly utilitarian and the cost is limited to the hardware.

Press your flowers and leaves between layers of absorbent paper or blank newsprint. You can reuse blotter paper indefinitely once it dries out. Shiny or heavily coated papers will not be absorbent enough to give a good result. Beware of colored or inky papers that will bleed dye onto the flowers. Also avoid embossed papers such as napkins or toweling that will impress little designs into the flowers and leaves.

Filling the Press

Just as with other methods of drying, the goal is to preserve as much of the natural color as you can and preserve materials quickly before they get moldy. Following the steps below will help to get the best possible result with roses or any other flower or leaf.

1   Gather plant material when it is dry. Avoid picking flowers or leaves after a rain or when they are wet with dew. Never mist flowers before pressing.

2   Pick whole flowers, petals, leaves, and buds. Pick flowers in different stages of development: buds, half-open, and fully open flowers. Select only "perfect" flowers and leaves for pressing; flowers don't improve in the press.

3   In the open press place two layers of blotting paper, then a layer of flowers or leaves, then another two pieces of paper, then another layer of flowers. Most presses will hold five or six layers of flowers. End with two more layers of paper and the top layer of wood. Tighten the wing nuts as much as you can. All of the plant materials in one layer should be of the same thickness. Put all the leaves in one layer, all the buds in one layer, and so on.

4   Retighten the press *every day*. As the flowers dry and moisture evaporates, there will be space between the layers. If you don't continue to tighten the press every day, the materials may wrinkle as they dry. For a really tight press, turn the wing nuts as far as you can, then put the whole press on the floor and sit on it to tighten it a few final turns. I never feel so pleased with my body weight as when I use it to assist in the tightening process.

5   After the third day, change the blotter paper and replace with fresh, dry paper. This step is critical to prevent mildew and browning if you are drying whole roses or other thick flowers. Carefully lift each flower or leaf with a knife and reposition it on a new paper layer. This process is akin to changing a baby's diaper to prevent a rash.

6   How do you know when the materials are dry? There's no harm in peeking. How fast they dry depends on the thickness of the flowers, their moisture content, how densely you pack each layer, the absorbency of the paper, and the warmth and humidity of the room where you store the press (remember warm and dry is always better). When you change the paper, flowers dry about 75 percent faster. When fully dry, flowers and leaves should feel papery and make a rustling noise.

7   Store pressed flowers between layers of wax paper in a cardboard box away from light and humidity, the two banes of all dried flowers.

8   If you do resort to the old methods and use a phone book for pressing a few favorite flowers, stack other books on top to weigh it down and switch the flowers to another book or at least drier pages after three days.

Pressing Roses

Pressed rose leaves are attractive in any picture, whether you use the rose flowers or not. They retain their rich, green color and form, and the serrated edges and veins are particularly attractive. Ivy, fern, cosmos, and rose leaves are my four favorite types of foliage for pressing. See pp. 45–47, the Quilting Bee, where pressed rose leaves were used with air-dried roses.

Rose flowers are harder to press because of their thickness. Thick flowers are slow to give up their moisture and thus have a tendency to mildew or change color before they dry. There are several solutions.

1   Remove the petals carefully and press the petals rather than the whole flower.

2   Press your smaller roses, not huge grandifloras, or roses with fewer petals.

3   If you must press larger roses, change the paper twice rather than once. In any case, remove the stems before pressing any rose. If you need stems in your finished picture, air-dry them separately.

Beyond the Garden

As with drying roses using other techniques, the original color of the rose largely determines how attractive the pressed form will be and how long the color will hold. White or cream roses have a tendency to turn beige, deep-red roses will always turn "black," the palest pink and yellow will quickly fade. I prefer to press roses with more vibrant colors: golden yellow, flame orange, and hot pink will produce gorgeous pressed roses.

TIPS:

Press more roses than you think you'll need for your project. You'll want to discard any crinkled or broken pieces after pressing.

Select a variety of flowers for an interesting picture, placing each variety on its own layer in the press.

Look for tiny weeds, grasses, and tendrils; sometimes stamens add interest to a picture.

If using a large seedpod or rose hip, slice it and press the slices.

Drying in Desiccants

Desiccants are materials such as sand, silica gel, cat box litter, and cornmeal that can absorb moisture from plant tissues. I've tried all of these materials and by far the best of these is silica gel, which is a white, sandlike material packaged for floral use. It's not cheap, but you can reuse it over and over by drying it when it becomes saturated. Manufacturers of craft silica gel mix colored particles in with the silica gel as moisture indicators. These particles are blue when dry, pink when saturated. After many uses, these colors disappear—I know not where—but by then you are so experienced in knowing how often to redry the silica that you no longer need an indicator.

One caveat: while there is no label on the package regarding dust masks (respirators), I wear one when I'm working with silica gel and you should too.

Preparing the Flowers

Cut stems off roses about a half-inch below the base of the flower.

The leaves can be pressed or dried in silica gel separately. Save the stems to air-dry for future use. If you know that you'll want the flowers to make a long-stemmed arrangement, slip a five-inch piece of thin wire through the ovary (the thick swelling at the base of the flower right above the stem) and let it extend out on each side. You will use this later to reattach the dried stems.

Using Silica Gel

All brands of silica gel for craft use include instructions, but here are some pointers. Find a plastic or metal container with tight-fitting lid, something wide and fairly shallow. Spread a layer of silica gel on the bottom, then place the flowers upright, leaving at least one-half inch between each flower and between the flowers and the edges of the container.

Use a two-cup liquid measure or other container with a pouring lip to transfer the silica gel around the flowers while controlling the flow. Gradually pour the silica gel around the outside of the flower, building up a ring that will support the petals and prevent them from flattening out. After this ring is built up, begin to pour the gel closer to the center of the flower until all petals are completely covered by about an inch of silica gel. If you have funnel- or pouch-shaped flowers, filling the centers with the silica first helps them hold their shapes as they are drying.

If the silica gel is relatively dry when you started, your flowers will be ready in one to two weeks. Fortunately it doesn't do them any harm if you forget them for a few months. When ready to use, gently pour off the silica gel and save it for another day. Blow off any silica crystals that have adhered to the flowers or use a dry, delicate paintbrush to brush the sandy stuff off the petals. If the flowers were free of moisture when they were buried, this will be very easy to do. If you get clumping on the flowers, it's a sign that they had drops of water on them when you started.

Reusing Silica Gel

After using any desiccant several times, it will have absorbed lots of moisture from the flowers and need to be dried again. In silica gel, the telltale crystals will turn from blue to pink. Pour the gel into a shallow baking pan, place the uncovered pan in a 200-degree oven, and stir every twenty minutes or so. Check after an hour to see if the crystals are yet blue. Remove from the oven and cover it with foil to prevent the gel from reabsorbing moisture from the humid air of your kitchen while it is cooling. Store in a tightly closed container until you're ready to use it again.

Beyond the Garden

Using Desiccant-Dried Flowers

Roses air-dry extremely well, but drying them in a desiccant keeps the flower structure looking more perfect. With flowers such as calla lilies, orchids, iris, tulips, and lilies, there is little choice but to use a desiccant. They lose their structure completely if hung to air-dry, so to preserve them at home, pressing or a desiccant are the only feasible methods. Wedding bouquets and other keepsake flowers in mixed bouquets must be taken apart to dry. Then you can treat each type of flower appropriately, pressing ferns and other foliage, air-drying the roses, and drying the lilies in a desiccant.

If you're not using them immediately, place the dried flowers in a single layer in a covered container. When making your design, tape any needed stems to the wires or wire the flowers directly to a wreath. You can also attach stems with hot glue if you prefer. Before adding desiccant-dried flowers to a wreath or arrangement, apply a protective spray such as a petal sealer or hair spray over the back and front surfaces, helping to seal out humidity. Spray from about fifteen inches away so you don't blast the flowers apart or apply a high shine. Three light coats are much more effective than one heavy coat. For more detailed instructions see *Harvesting, Preserving, and Arranging Dried Flowers* by Cathy Miller.

Drying Roses in a Microwave

You can, but why would you want to? You can only process one or two flowers at a time, you're bound to toast or cook a few, and the results with roses are not as pleasing as either air-drying or drying in silica gel. Articles on microwave drying generally recommend burying them in silica gel before giving the flowers a zap, and if you're going to all that trouble for one rose at a time, why not be patient and wait a week for perfect flowers to emerge from the desiccant "naturally"?

A NOTE ABOUT FREEZE-DRIED ROSES

You can't do it at home. Freeze-drying is not a process for the home freezer, but for a very expensive machine. It vacuums out the water quickly at a low temperature and is economical only for businesses that process thousands of flowers for the wholesale market. All freeze-dried materials are then coated with a variety of chemicals to keep the water from reabsorbing. Freeze-dried roses are beautiful but fragile and can be purchased at upscale florists and shops specializing in aroma products.

Freeze-dried roses look almost perfect.

Roses Preserved

Color Me Beautiful

Fresh roses have luminous colors, whether pink as soft as the inside of a baby's ear or hottest fuchsia, pastel peach or hot orange, and as many shades of white as Sherman-Williams's paints. Light bounces off each petal, each shade and tint gleams. Each has its uses and its champions in the garden and in the home.

Not so with dried roses. Light no longer reflects but seems to be gobbled up by the dried flowers. Without the glisten, without the faint iridescence, when even the structure changes somewhat, color and aroma predominate. No matter what you do, deep reds in roses such as 'Mr. Lincoln' turn almost black in the drying process. White or cream colored roses quickly fade to a dead shade of beige.

But if you begin with the right shades you will be rewarded. Don't bother drying white roses unless they're in your wedding bouquet. You may want to rethink the choice of colors for the bouquet if you have your heart set on preserving it. All flowers will gradually fade over time but will allow you years—even decades—of enjoyment if you start with bright colors, rather than the months you will have if you start with the palest pastels. Use bright yellow-gold, bright orange, hot pink, flaming reds, and rich purples. Leave tints like chocolate for fresh flower bouquets.

Sunlight and humidity are anathemas to any dried flower. Colors fade quickly when either factor is present. So do what you can to avoid both. Place keepsake flowers under glass or away from sunny windows. Keep out of steamy bathrooms. Or be prepared to dry new roses and make new arrangements every year—by no means a terrible fate.

Handling Dried Roses

Roses and most other flowers shrink as the water leaves the petals and stems. The petals and leaves become more wrinkled and lose some of their original shape. Flattening in a press and drying in a desiccant are two methods that try to overcome these difficulties. Pressed rose leaves are perfectly well shaped, albeit two-dimensional. Rose flowers dried in silica gel look almost fresh and still retain some of the original aroma, but the process is a bit of a bother. Air-drying is still the technique preferred by many people even though flowers collapse inward while hanging.

Here's a technique I've developed for enhancing the shape of air-dried roses just before using them in an arrangement.

Steaming

1   Put water in a teakettle and bring to a rolling boil.

2   Hold an air-dried rose in one hand about eight inches from the flower head. If your kettle has a whistling device, hold that open with the other hand.

3   Hold the flower with the face straight on into the steam, about an inch away from the spout. **KEEP YOUR HAND OFF TO THE SIDE AND AWAY FROM THE DIRECT PATH OF THE STEAM TO AVOID BURNS.** This is very easy to do if you pay attention. Hold in place five to ten seconds. Watch the petals: you'll see them slowly start to open like in slow-motion photography.

4   When this starts to happen, take the rose away from the steam and gently open the petals. You may have to repeat the steam treatment one more time, then continue opening the flower by hand.

5   The flower will dry again in less than five minutes away from the steam, and it will always retain the new shape, which is quite realistic. Blossoms will be very close to their original size and very appealing. Use in any arrangement.

Yes, I've said that humidity is the bane of dried flowers, but this process is so brief that it seems to have no ill effects.

Roses Preserved

Pairs of air-dried roses. The left rose of each pair has been steamed open. Notice the size differential.

Caring for Roses Designs

All dried flowers fade fast in direct sunlight and high humidity. They are also delicate and can't stand frequent fondling and touching. That said, find a good spot in your home for placing your finished wreath, arrangement, topiary, or potpourri. If you must have a bowl of rose pot-pourri on your windowsill, resign yourself to bleached colors and diminished aroma or be prepared to replace it in a few months. A dining room table is a good spot for a dried arrangement. It's often in the center of a room, well away from sunny windows. If the table is used infre-quently, the delicate arrangement doesn't get shifted around too often. A shelf or mantel are other practical spots for dried arrangements.

Fresh roses last longer in a cool spot, away from sunlight, which fades the flowers but also away from chilling breezes or drafts, which dry out the petals.

Long-Term Care: Dusting

For fresh roses, care is a simple matter. Add fresh water. Remove brown petals. Cut out any dying foliage. Enjoy the arrangement and discard when the aesthetic appeal is gone.

For dried roses, long-term care involves dusting, and dusting is no easy matter.

Here are three ways to deal with the matter.

1   Take the arrangement outside. Carefully invert it while holding the floral foam or other mechanics in place as best you can. Tap the bottom of the container or the back of the wreath a few times and the dust will fly away along with any broken floral pieces.

2   Less effective is a hair dryer, set on low, which will gently blow the dust away. Dusters often get carried away and put the nozzle too close to the design, blowing away some flowers in the ensuing tornado.

3   Discard. With potpourris, this is the only recourse for dusty materials.

Beyond the Garden

Epilogue

I've designed and written specific instructions, almost recipes, for some beautiful arrangements with roses in a starring or supporting role. I hope you have great pleasure constructing or displaying one or several of these designs. You'll take pride in what you make, whether it is for yourself or a gift.

The greatest pleasure of all comes from personalizing a design. A different color range, a different size, several different ingredients, and suddenly it's yours, not mine. You won't have the exact containers that I did, you may have other flowers growing in your garden or other favorites at the florist. By all means branch out and see where your own creativity takes you.

Like many of the beginning students in my floral design classes, you may start by trying to copy and then find you like your variation a lot better. Terrific!

*A bit of frangrance always
clings to the hand that gives you roses.*

— Chinese proverb

Appendix I:

Bibliography

Black, Penny. *The Book of Potpourri.* New York: Simon and Schuster, 1989.

Brickell, Christopher and Judith D. Zuk, eds. *The American Horticultural Society A–Z Encyclopedia of Garden Plants.* New York: DK Publishing Inc., 1996.

Davis, Esther. *Sensational Dried Flowers.* Emmaus, Penn.: Rodale Press, 1999.

Platt, Ellen Spector. *Flower Crafts.* Emmaus, Penn.: Rodale Press, 1993.

Platt, Ellen Spector. *The Ultimate Wreath Book.* Emmaus, Penn.: Rodale Press, 1995.

Rhode, Eleanour Sinclair, *Rose Recipes from Olden Times.* New York: Dover Publications, 1973.

Rosenfeld, Lois G. *The Garden Tourist.* New York: The Garden Tourist Press, 2002.

Schorr, Phil, ed. *Handbook for Selecting Roses.* Shreveport, La.: American Rose Society, 2003.

Appendix II:

Rose Gardens

There are hundreds of public rose gardens in the United States and Canada, some in public parks, some in botanic gardens and arboreta, some surrounding historic homes, museums, or libraries. Yet others are self-contained and were developed as display or test gardens by rose societies. As their purposes vary, so do their aesthetic appeal and their research value for the home gardener. If you want help deciding which roses to purchase for your home, visit a garden near you. In June the sights and scents are glorious. If you can go again right after a heavy rain or in an August drought or heat wave, you'll be able to see the roses at their worst, which is a great help in deciding what to plant. To find a rose garden near you, search the American Rose Society or Canadian Rose Society Web sites listed below in Appendix III.

Lois G. Rosenfeld, author of *The Garden Tourist,* generously described some of her favorites as did other colleagues who write about gardens in the United States and Canada. I've included my own top picks as well.

East

Colonial Park Arboretum
van der Goot Rose Garden
Somerset County, NJ
(732) 873-2459
www.park.co.somerset.NJ.us
This rose garden contains 3,000 roses with several hundred varieties and displays of AARS winners, as well as a fragrance and sensory garden.

Cranford Rose Garden
Brooklyn Botanic Garden
Brooklyn, NY
(718) 622-4433
www.bbg.org
Established in 1927, this award-winning, magnificent sunken garden specializes in species roses; old garden roses such as eglantines, bourbons, China, and moss roses; hardy modern roses; miniatures; and sprawling climbers.

Dag Hammarskjold Gardens at the United Nations
New York, NY
(212) 963-1234
www.un.org
More than twenty-five award-winning roses with spring bulbs and espaliered trees. The setting can't be matched.

Elizabeth Park
Hartford, CT
(860) 242-0017
Fifteen thousand rose bushes in a garden more than one hundred years old.

Hershey Gardens
Hershey, PA
(717) 534-3492
www.hersheygardens.com
An award-winning rose garden started in 1937, it now includes other display gardens as well.

West

Balboa Park
San Diego, CA
(619) 235-1100
www.balboapark.org
A unique urban park with many gardens, museums, a zoo, Moorish architecture, and the award-winning Inez Grant Parker Memorial Rose Garden.

Huntington Library
Art Collections and Botanical
Gardens, San Marino, CA
(near Pasadena)
(626) 405-2100
www.huntington.org
This 150-acre botanical garden surrounds the library and museum. The rose garden is a highlight along with the Japanese garden.

International Rose Test Garden
Portland, OR
(503) 796-5193
Eighty-five hundred roses displayed in the "City of Roses."

Portland, Oregon, International
Rose Test Garden at the Hoyt
Arboretum
(503) 823-3636
www.parks.ci.portland.or.us
Eight thousand roses in the oldest public rose garden in the United States. Also visit the Sunken Rose Garden at Peninsula Park (same contact numbers).

North

Butchart Gardens
Victoria, BC, Canada
(250) 652-5256
www.butchartgardens.com
Delightful design for a rose garden in a limited space, with other roses incorporated in beds throughout.

Minter Gardens
Chilliwack, BC, Canada
(888) 646-8377
www.minter.org
A somewhat small but stunning display.

Montreal Botanical Gardens
(Jardin Botanique du Montreal)
Montreal, QC, Canada
(514) 872-1400
www.ville.montreal.qc.ca/jardin
Ten thousand roses bloom in the garden from May until October. They're planted in a lovely setting of shrubs and trees.

Royal Botanical Gardens
Hamilton, ON, Canada
(near Toronto)
(905) 527-1158
www.rbg.ca
An extensive rose garden, with an excellent display of climbers and miniature roses, among others.

South

The Garden of the American Rose
Center
Shreveport, LA
(318) 983-5402
www.ars.org
More than forty acres of roses, including award winners; test gardens; special events; and educational programs.

Tyler Municipal Rose Garden and
Rose Museum
Tyler, TX
(903) 597-3130
www.tylertexas.com
Tyler, Texas, is called "the rose capital of the nation" and "the city of roses" because growers in the county supply about one-fifth of the nation's commercially produced bushes. Tyler has the largest municipal rose garden in the country with about 40,000 roses and 500 varieties. There is also a rose museum and an annual rose festival in the fall, supported by local growers who also founded the Texas Rose research foundation.

Appendix

Appendix III:

Rose Societies and Organizations

All-America Rose Selections Inc. (AARS)
(312) 552-4400
www.rose.org
AARS has twenty-seven trial gardens around the United States and Canada to test roses in various regions and 133 public gardens where enthusiasts can view the winners. Well labeled and cared for, the roses in these trial gardens feature past and current winners, new roses on trial, yet-to-be-named winners for next year, as well as other top roses. Past winners still considered classics are 'Peace,' 1946; 'Tropicana,' 1963; and 'Mr. Lincoln,' 1965.

Search for a public rose garden or test trial garden near you on the Web site. It will also provide information on rose gardening and where to buy winners.

American Rose Society (ARS)
(318) 938-5402
www.ars.org
The American Rose Society Web site includes a database of rosarians who are willing to answer questions from neighbors about growing roses. You will also find listings of international, national, and local rose shows and Rose Society chapters in your area. The ARS is the largest society for a single flower in the country, founded in 1892. They offer many valuable publications. Join the society online or by phone.

Canadian Rose Society (CRS)
(416) 466-1879
www.mirror.org/groups/crs
The easy-to-use Web site lists chapters of the Canadian Rose Society; local, regional, and national events and rose shows; links to other international societies in Japan, Australia, and throughout Europe; public gardens throughout Canada that specialize in roses; and Canadian rose growers. You will also find resources on roses for cold climates, including Zones 2 and 3.

Appendix IV:

Catalogs and Web Sources

Antique Rose Emporium
Brenham, TX
(800) 441-0002
www.weAREroses.com
The Antique Rose Emporium specializes in more than one hundred old roses on their own roots, with historic parentage and date of introduction.

Arena Roses
Pasa Robles, CA
(805) 227-4094
www.arenaroses.com
Beware of this catalog: it contains the most lush, enticing photos and descriptions of flowers. The rose-lovers lexicon in the back of the catalog is extremely helpful for novices, as is their comparison of rose shapes. Arena Roses carries antique roses and new roses of all types, as well as tree roses, both standard and weeping.

Beyond the Garden

David Austin Roses
Tyler, TX and Albrighton, England
(800) 328-8893
www.davidaustinroses.com
David Austin Roses is known for its new roses in the old tradition, crosses between antique roses, tree roses, and modern teas and floribunda, also called English roses, which are fragrant, hardy, and combine some of the best old and new qualities. The company also carries interesting categories such as climbers for trees and unsightly buildings, thornless roses, English roses for hot climates (Zones 9–10) and cold areas (Zone 4).

Heirloom Roses
St. Paul, OR
(503) 538-1576
www.heirloomroses.com
A catalog to curl up with. Lovely categories for all needs including roses for small gardens, roses for woodland plantings, roses for cut flowers, special fragrances, and many more. If you crave a rose that smells like green apples, white hyacinth, raspberry, lily-of-the-valley, or myrrh, don't miss this list. Specializing in virus-free roses.

Jackson & Perkins
Medford, OR
(800) 292-4769
www.jacksonandperkins.com
Old and reliable rose growers now also selling perennials.

Nor'East Miniature Roses
Rowley, MA
(800) 426-6485
www.noreast-miniroses.com
Catalog of miniatures for beds and borders, hanging baskets, and containers, including Hall of Fame winners from the American Rose Society.

Old Heirloom Roses
Halifax, NS, Canada
(902) 471-3364
Old Heirloom Roses carries organically grown, hardy bushes for Zones 4–6. They also produce a newsletter.

Pickering Nurseries
Pickering, ON, Canada
(905) 839-2111
www.pickeringnurseries.com
Pickering Nurseries offers a great selection of antique roses such as albas, bourbons, damascenas, gallicas, musk, and moss roses as well as modern roses. Their roses, grown in Canada, are winter hardy in northern areas of the United States. They list roses with outstanding hips, a favorite category of mine. The paper catalog is somewhat difficult to use.

Roses Unlimited
Laurens, SC
(864) 682-7673
www.rosesunlimiteddownroot.com
A favorite source for many rosarians for the wide variety of root roses.

Roses of Yesterday
Watsonville, CA
(831) 728-1901
www.rosesofyesterday.com
Old, rare, unusual, and selected modern roses are this company's specialty. There is also a display garden on site.

Appendix

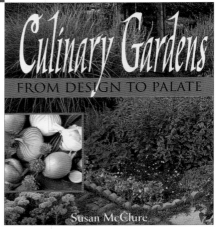